Sleeping Baby, Happy Parents

Simple steps to great baby sleep

By Emma Thomson

Introduction

Reading this book and following some of the tips and guidance will help you and your baby get a good night's sleep. Good sleep is fundamental to your physical and mental wellbeing. We wanted you to have all the information you need to make confident parenting choices.

We start by focusing on you and your wellbeing before looking at your baby's perspective of the world. We describe how much your little human's environment has changed, and it has changed a lot! We explore parenting styles and what kind of parent you want to be. This is followed by looking at the sleep environment and how to make sure the one you design is both safe and conducive to your baby's needs. This will set the scene for good naps and a great night's sleep.

Preparing your baby for sleep, understanding sleep cues, soothing your baby and creating routines are all described allowing you to pick and try what you think will work best for you. Sleep training can be a controversial subject. We describe the most widely accepted techniques helping you to select the type you want and which suits your parenting style best. Creating a good sleep plan is key to you and your baby getting good quality sleep. Your sleep plan works best if it is created by you and your partner so that it is well understood and followed by you both.

The quick fix sleep solutions in the last chapter gives many ideas and tips on what to do for you and your baby in order to quickly take control and just get some precious sleep!

I spent over ten years as an antenatal teacher supporting expectant and new parents while being mum to three (average sleeping) children of my own. I have shared my experiences about what worked best for me with my babies. I also wanted to share my knowledge and experience as well as the latest research and thinking on how to get your baby to enjoy good quality sleep.

Being a parent should be the most wonderful time in your life. Having a young baby is a very short phase and should be enjoyed while it lasts. You will only enjoy it if you are getting enough sleep. Hopefully reading this book will have provided all you need to make good choices to get good quality sleep. This will help create great memories of this precious time which are lovely to reflect on when the teenage years kick in!

To keep this book short, simple and easy to read it is written as though you are the mother and your baby is a boy.

Contents

Chapter 1: Think About You First

Let's begin with you, the primary care provider. It may seem strange to begin a book about baby sleep, by talking about you. However, in order to help both you and your baby sleep better, it is important to understand the roles you both play in getting a good night's sleep.

In the next chapter, we will look at life from your baby's perspective. First we need to understand how life is for you right now and the possible impact your baby is having on your sleep. Your wellbeing, state of mental and physical health affects how well you are able to cope with the demands and challenges of a young baby. If you are the mother, father, or primary care provider; how well you feel directly translates in to how well you cope. If you are calm and happy, your baby is much more likely to be calm and happy. A calm and happy baby will be much easier to settle down to sleep and will sleep for longer. This is not rocket science and a very logical process for most healthy babies. However, it is very easy to forget the impact your emotional state has on your baby when you are so busy being a new parent. There is a tendency to place all the emphasis on 'sorting' your baby without making sure you are sorted first.

Why does it matter if I am calm or not?

When your baby is born, his or her brain is still underdeveloped. Many of the higher 'thinking' parts of their brain mature as a result of interactions with you and other important adults in their life. Your baby's brain systems for coping with fear, anger and separation are examples of these underdeveloped systems.

Emotionally responsive parenting helps your baby form vital connections in his brain which enable him to cope with his feelings. These include the ability to calm himself when he is upset. Your emotional state has a direct and powerful impact on the emotional systems in your baby's brain and body. There is an important flow of emotional energy from your brain to your baby's brain and from your body to your baby's body. Depending on your emotional state, this flow of energy will create different responses in your baby. It makes sense therefore that if you are calm, relaxed and happy, you will handle, hold and interact with your baby in a calm and relaxed way. You are more likely to use loving facial expressions, eye contact and speak to your baby in a tone of voice which is also calming. Its logical that consistent treatment like this will ultimately result in a calmer baby. Of course, the opposite is also true. If you are struggling to stay calm when you interact with your baby, it will be much more difficult for him to develop and activate his own calm response. Don't panic though, we all have good and bad moments. Being the parent to a baby is very challenging and can be stressful especially when you are feeling sleep deprived. The important thing is to make sure you have more calm interactions overall with your baby than stressed ones.

If you are struggling to be or stay calm, you need to address this. Reading this chapter will help you to understand why you might be finding it difficult and provide guidance on how to manage better. You can also read *quick tips for calming yourself* at the end of this chapter.

How are you feeling right now?

Although it may seem impossible to get headspace to think about anything other than your baby's next feed or change, it's important to invest some time in yourself. This will reap big rewards. The first step is to carry out a quick review of where you are now.

If you are the mother, ask yourself these two questions:

1. How is your physical health?

The physical discomfort that women go through during the last stages of pregnancy can seem insignificant compared to the birthing process, especially if you experienced birth interventions. Even if your experience was straightforward, your body needs time to heal and recover. Don't forgot your body was adapting and changing for nine months. It is reasonable to expect it will take the same time to return to its pre-pregnancy state. After birth a bruised perineum, healing wounds and sore nipples, to name but a few, can all lead to physical discomfort. Even if the birth was some time ago for you, residual pain and niggles can linger for some women. It is therefore important to do something about it. If you had to compare your physical health before you were pregnant and now, what would you score out of 10? (Higher is better). If your score is 7 or below, make the time to contact your relevant health professional and arrange an appointment to see them. Get advice about how to help yourself as soon as possible. This is not an endurance test and delaying is not going to help you or your baby and certainly will not help you to sleep or cope better.

2. How is your mood?

Pregnancy and birth are often described as an emotional rollercoaster. Our hormones get a lot of bad press as the instigators of our changing moods but really they are amazing. We would not have a pregnancy or a baby without them doing their job. Our hormones are responsible for many changes during pregnancy and after birth and tend to result in some emotional upheaval. This is sometimes called the baby blues and is experienced by fifty to eighty percent of new mothers. The baby blues may last anywhere between a few days to a week or two after giving birth. Symptoms can include crying, anxiety, sadness, irritability, mood swings, reduced appetite, trouble concentrating, and trouble sleeping.

Baby blues and postpartum depression (US term) or postnatal depression (UK term) are quite similar, but they usually differ in the duration as well as intensity. While there is no single cause of baby blues or postpartum (postnatal) depression, physical and emotional changes can play a role in its development. Many other factors can also contribute such as anxiety about your ability to take care of your baby, feeling you've lost your identity or the ability to control your life.

Baby blues that last longer than two weeks is considered to be postpartum (postnatal) depression. Moreover, if the symptoms of the baby blues are so intense that they interfere with your ability to care for your infant or to perform daily activities, the condition is considered postpartum (postnatal) depression even if the symptoms happen in less than two weeks.

The symptoms are varied and are different for everyone. They usually develop within the first few weeks although depression can occur anytime in the first year after birth. Symptoms can include severe mood swings, loss of appetite, overeating, excessive crying, anger, intense irritability, severe anxiety, panic attacks, difficulty bonding with your baby, and in some extreme instances, thoughts of harming yourself or your baby. From this books perspective, common symptoms of the condition also include; inability to sleep or oversleeping and overwhelming fatigue or loss of energy.

New mothers can also suffer from anxiety related to other issues such as financial or relationship problems and career issues. There tends to also be an unrealistic expectation that today's mothers should be superwomen, being able to do everything; having a job, taking care of the children, managing a household and having an active social life. It's easy to feel the pressure of doing everything for everyone but not looking after yourself.

If you are the father:

Did you know that just as many men suffer from postpartum or postnatal depression as women? Although you have not experienced changes in your hormones, you may have found witnessing your partner's pregnancy journey difficult to watch, without the ability to really share some of the changes. It may also be that your partner giving birth was very traumatic, or perhaps there is a health issue with your new baby. In addition to this many of the factors that contribute to depression are the same for men and women. For example, worries over finances, housing, your relationship or becoming a parent.

Whether you are reading this as the mother, father, or primary care provider and any of this sounds like it might apply to you, then you need to do something about it. When thinking about your emotional health, it is important to remember that we all have good and bad days. To gain a perspective, it's useful to think about how you've felt over a period of time. Try thinking back over the last weeks and months to understand how you've felt in general. If you feel your mood has been persistently low (and this is different to your normal disposition) then it's time to get some help. Make an appointment with your health care provider. They are trained to deal with these types of conditions and will be able to give advice about how to look after yourself. Depression connected with pregnancy and birth is a complex issue which is thought to affect up to fifty percent of the population. Most go unreported as often parents struggle on and eventually get better. (It is not the intention of this book to cover all aspects of this condition but more to give an overview to help you decide on what action to take).

Many new parents fall in to a 'grey area' where they feel their mood may be low but they are not considered clinically depressed. If you feel in this place, you should do as much as possible to help yourself. This is so important because you are the parent or primary care provider of a young baby, whose interactions will influence how your baby's brain will develop and form. It is therefore very important to ensure that you are looking after yourself properly.

Things to do to help yourself

Now that you more fully appreciate how important it is to take care of yourself, it's time to look at specific and practical actions that you can do.

Accept offers of help: Even as recently as our own great grandmothers, it was expected that new mothers would spend a period of time resting in bed after birth while being looked after by family and friends. In traditional cultures a period of 'lying in' is normal after birth and this can last for many days and sometimes weeks. This allows new mothers to recover from birth, slowly adjust to their new role and get to know their baby. Nowadays it is expected that new mothers will jump out of bed and get back to 'normal' right away. This is unrealistic for most. Make sure you accept offers of help whenever they are made. Ask people for help if they don't offer. It is not a sign of weakness but common sense. Your primary role is to learn to be a mother to your new baby, not to have an empty laundry basket. Postnatal doulas and maternity nurses are a good alternative if you don't have help readily available.

Learn relaxation or calming techniques: If you attended birth preparation classes, you will likely have learned some relaxation and breathing techniques for birth. These techniques are designed to help you relax and manage birth in a calm way. Relaxed breathing can be just as useful when coping with the demands and challenges of a young baby. If you'd like to try something new or different, there are many apps and downloads available which teach you how to use your breathing to relax. Why not listen to some of these during your baby's feeds as practice and then you can test out the technique next time you feel stressed? This won't be wasted time. Practicing this skill will be invaluable in the future when you need to stay calm as you experience the ups and downs of raising your wonderful child to adulthood.

Take naps: Although this is common (and very sensible) advice, for many women, it is difficult to follow. Often when their baby naps, their instinct is to jump up and get the chores done first. If this sounds like you, why not compromise and rest first and if your baby has a longer nap, use the additional time to catch up on chores. Of course, if you have other children at home, this will make napping impossible. Instead, while the baby sleeps, make this a quiet time for you and your older child instead. Lie down on your bed or snuggle up on the sofa. Read quietly or watch something calm on TV.

Eat the right stuff: Giving birth and taking care of a newborn demands a great deal from new parents so it's essential to fuel up with good food. Don't be tempted to skip meals or go for empty carbs. Fill up on whole, nutritious foods like grains, nuts, vegetables, and fruits. It's also very important that you get enough iron in your diet. A lack of iron can make you feel very tired and low levels can eventually lead to anemia. If you don't feel like eating full meals, eat small amounts more frequently. Be sure to stay hydrated, especially if you're breastfeeding. If you have no time to prepare food or cook, ask friends and family to bring round a meal that is quick to reheat. You can return the favour in the future.

Exercise: Exercise should be part of your routine and studies show it is a key way to improve your mood. Exercise also offers plenty of other benefits, such as speeding up the after-birth recovery for mothers, reducing fatigue, stress, anxiety, and tension. Exercise also increases strength, flexibility, and energy levels, as well as improving muscle tone, digestion, circulation, and importantly your sleep patterns.

Note, not all types of exercise are safe for women to do right after giving birth. If you are still in the early weeks, you can start off with pelvic floor exercises, and walking. These can be done for both vaginal and caesarian births, but check with your doctor for the ideal duration and intensity of the exercises. You can gradually build up your exercise routine as you get back to normal. Sometimes it can seem impossible to fit exercise in to your day with everything else that needs done with a new baby. Start with something simple that you can do as a family such as taking your baby for a walk to the park or to visit friends. Starting a healthy lifestyle early in your baby's life will be invaluable for both your futures.

Reach out to other parents: Having a support group of other parents who know exactly what you're going through will help you in a whole range of ways. One of these ways is that other parents can give you valuable tips on child care and parenting. It's also great having someone listen to your worries that understands them and this alone is often enough to make you feel better. Moreover, you will find comfort in knowing that the physical and emotional changes you are experiencing are all normal and that they are temporary.

Treat yourself to "me" time: If you are the parent who is at home all day caring for your baby, it can be impossible to make any time for yourself. However, even ten minutes of "me" time can work wonders for your mental state. In the early days, use this time to meditate, take a nap, do some yoga, take a hot shower or relaxing bath, read a book, or any activity that makes you feel good about yourself. You can enjoy "me" time every day if you create a loose daily structure and enlist the help of your partner or an available family member. As your baby gets older, you can gradually increase this time to allow you to begin to reinstate some of your old hobbies, pastimes or exercise routines. Where possible you can also hire a babysitter or temporary help to let you and your partner enjoy important time together as a couple.

What's next?

Okay so we've not solved the sleep problem yet but hopefully you are beginning to appreciate the importance of looking after yourself in the context of helping you and your baby sleep better. Although it may seem impossible to imagine creating time to do anything except care for your baby, making a small space for yourself in the day is achievable. This is a short term situation as your baby is growing and maturing every day. A small investment of time now will help you to improve your physical and emotional health. Even if you are feeling happy and well, you deserve some regeneration time and this in turn will be invaluable for your baby's long term healthy development.

Quick tips for calming yourself

1. **Use relaxed breathing:** Sit down and take a few long, slow deep breaths to relax your body.

2. **Breathe fresh air:** Open a window and taking some deep breaths. Alternatively, go for a walk with your baby. Even short distances can settle your mind and help you both relax.

3. **Play music:** Listen to music which makes you feel happy and relaxed. Moving your body at the same time can help. Did you put together a playlist for your birth? Why not play that to make you smile.

4. **Eat or drink something:** Check when you last ate or had a drink. Your body needs fuel to manage itself well. It's easy to forget to eat or drink regularly when you are caring for a young baby.

5. **Get some space:** If you really feel stressed pass your baby to someone else while you get calm. If no one is available to help, gently lay your baby in a safe place such as its crib or cot until you feel calmer. Don't feel guilty. We all have our limits; the key is to recognize them.

6. **Phone a friend:** Talking is a great way to relieve stress. Why not arrange to speak to someone you really like and trust. A quick download will work wonders!

My experience.

With my first baby, I had a very long, slow labour which ended in an assisted delivery. It left me feeling physically exhausted and sore. Mentally, I felt slightly removed from reality and quite disorientated, like I was in a foggy world. I had very few friends who had babies and no family nearby. It was winter in Scotland when my son was born and the days were dark, cold and long. I had no transport and felt pretty lonely and isolated at home with a very small baby.

The thing that helped me most was getting out of the house and meeting other parents. I had made some friends through antenatal classes and met them on a regular basis. I also went to a baby and toddler group. Even though my son was still too young to take part, it was so helpful to speak to other mothers and feel normal. To truly relax I needed time away from my baby. For example, once a week my friend picked me up and we went to the pool for a swim. I found trying to relax at home more difficult as I could always hear my baby crying. Instinctively

I wanted to soothe him even if I was in another room and he was being looked after by someone else.

Chapter 2: It Helps to Understand Your Baby's Perspective

Many people embark on parenthood knowing that sleep deprivation is likely with a young baby, but few of us really understand the impact it will have on our lives. What we discover is that when our baby arrives we are not quite ready and many things about baby sleep are still unclear. This is not helped by the fact that all babies are unique and behave differently. It often seems as if other people's babies sleep more than our own. In this chapter, we aim to clarify some of this confusion and explain what a normal sleep pattern is for a baby and why this is so different to our own. In addition, we provide an insight in to what life is like from your baby's point of view.

Author of "The Happiest Baby on the Block", Harvey Karp, describes the period following birth and up to the end of the first three months of life, as the fourth trimester. Unlike other mammals, who are quickly able to walk, stay close to their mothers or cling on to her for survival, human babies need much longer to develop to this stage. Ideally human babies would remain inside their mothers for longer but due to female pelvis evolution, babies must make their way in to the world early, to fit through the pelvis.

In the fourth trimester, your tiny newborn has left the familiar comfort and noises of the warm, dark womb and moves to a bright environment full of unsettling new sights, sounds, smells, and sensations, as well as changing temperatures. This period of adjustment to the world outside your womb is a time of enormous change and development.

Even if your baby has passed the newborn stage, it is useful to understand the journey he has been on, giving you a good baseline of knowledge to work with.

Life on the outside – Your newborn's perspective

Previously we read about the importance of looking after yourself and the positive impact you can have on your baby when you feel calm and well. The next most important thing is to understand life from your baby's perspective. This valuable insight will help you gain a deeper understanding of how best to interact with your baby, stay calmer and feel more confident. This better understanding will also help you to form a deeper relationship with your baby and ultimately achieve better sleep experiences for you both.

As you would expect life inside and outside the womb is vastly different. It's hard for an adult to imagine quite how big this transition is for a baby (even though we've all done it)! One way to try to gain a small understanding of this change is to imagine how you would feel in the scenario below:

At very short notice, you've been assigned to work in a different country. It's impossible to be completely prepared. You arrive in a place with a different language, culture, food, time zone, and even climate. You feel a range of emotions. These include being very disorientated, frustrated, and a little scared at times. You also feel excited and happy at the new experience. You have little control over these changes and rely on others to help you. Over time, you begin to adjust to your new environment and gradually feel more relaxed.

Although this scenario is not the same as that of your baby's, it gives a small insight into their experience. Importantly, it highlights how much easier the transition is with the help and support of someone caring rather than having to cope alone.

Understanding your baby's journey will better equip you to help him adjust to life in the outside world more easily. The list below shows some of the basic differences that he will experience.

Sight

Inside the womb: A fetus can detect light inside its mother. The light is faint as it must travel through body fat, muscle and clothing.

Outside the womb: A newborn's vision is blurry but he can see up to ten inches away. (This is the approximate distance from the breast to his mother's face.) He can detect high-contrast hues, such as black and white, as well as primary colours.

Hearing

Inside the womb: As early as 20 weeks, your baby can detect sounds. The womb is noisy with the sounds of his mother's heartbeat, her rumbling digestive system and a garbled version of her voice. He can also hear muffled external sounds that are loud enough to reach him.

Outside the womb: A newborn can hear all sorts of sounds from his environment. These can be overwhelming for him at times.

Touch

Inside the womb: Your baby was held constantly by your womb, enveloped by warm water.

Outside the womb: Your baby experiences a whole range of sensations in his environment. He likes to feel a loving touch best.

Taste and hunger

Inside the womb: Your baby was fed constantly through the placenta and never felt hunger.

Outside the womb: A newborn needs to cry for food when he is hungry. He relies completely on someone else to feed him. He can taste sweet and bitter although he likes sweet tastes such as breast milk best.

Smell

Inside the womb: Your baby can smell by 'breathing', and swallowing his amniotic fluid which surrounds him. The fluid contains the smells and flavours of the foods you are eating.

Outside the womb: A newborn baby has a very sensitive nose. He is already familiar with his mother's scent and is comforted by it. Strong smells can be very overpowering to him.

Temperature

Inside the womb: The temperature inside the womb always stays constant.

Outside the womb: A newborn is exposed to a range of different temperatures. At birth he is not fully able to regulate his own body temperature. This needs to be managed by his care provider through appropriate clothing, bedding and room temperature adjustments.

Sleep

Inside the womb: Your baby sleeps whenever he wants, but he is able to take sleep cues from his mother. This means he can be more active during the day when she is awake, and calmer at night when she is less active. He also receives his mother's hormones through the placenta and they can help guide him towards a day and night pattern.

Outside the womb: A newborn's sleeping pattern is influenced by his hunger. His stomach is so tiny (the size of a marble at birth) that he needs regular feeds. Initially, he has no concept of day and night but will learn this as he matures. (For reference, an average adults stomach is the size of their clenched fist.)

I'm sure you'll agree that there is a lot going on in your baby's life! Let's focus more closely now on your baby's sleep pattern and answer two very important questions:

1. How much sleep do babies need?
2. Why are adult and baby sleep patterns so different?

1. How much sleep do babies need?
Babies have so much new information to process and are growing and developing at such a fast pace, they need a lot of sleep.

The longitudinal study published by Iglowstein and colleagues in 2003 is still very relevant today. In it almost five hundred Swiss children were observed from birth to sixteen years to identify their sleep patterns. The results for the first twelve months of their life are shown below. You should use these figures as an approximate guide on how much sleep your baby needs.

The following shows the total duration babies slept during a twenty four hour period, which includes both daytime and night time sleep.

At 1 month, on average babies slept for 14 to 15 hours.

At 3 months, on average babies also slept 14 to 15 hours.

At 6 months, on average babies slept for 14.2 hours.

At 9 months, the average was very similar at 13.9 hours.

At 12 months, the average was the same, 13.9 hours.

What you can see is that the total number of hours of sleep varied very little from a one month baby to a twelve month baby. The big difference however, is how the hours are consolidated. A one month old wakes regularly every few hours to feed. By the time your baby is twelve months old, their sleep pattern has changed significantly and matches an adults much more closely.

2. Why is adult and baby sleep so different?
Babies need to sleep for many hours during a twenty four hour period. Unfortunately, (and especially during the fourth trimester) this sleep is not all together in one long continuous sleep. As adults we have a long sleep at night and are awake during the day. Initially, a baby has no awareness of day and night, waking and sleeping is primarily driven by their need to eat regularly. An infant's stomach is just tiny (marble sized at birth) therefore they must waken to be fed. As their stomachs grow and mature, they are able to eat more and therefore can sleep for longer periods. In addition to this, your baby's sleep cycle is initially quite different to your own.

How is my baby's sleep different to mine?

Adult sleep cycles

These last about ninety to one hundred minutes in which the average adult moves through five stages of sleep. These include four stages of deep or non-rapid eye movement (NREM) sleep and a fifth stage of active or rapid eye movement (REM) sleep, when most dreaming takes place. At the end of each cycle, you would either wake up or repeat the cycle.

Baby sleep cycles

During the first nine months of life, an average baby moves through only two stages of sleep. These last about fifty to sixty minutes and move from active to quiet sleep. In babies, active sleep, (the equivalent of REM sleep), comes first. While in active sleep, babies exhibit fluttering eyelids, occasional body movements, vocalizations, such as brief cries or grunts, and relatively rapid, irregular breathing. This is the sleep stage where babies are more easily awakened. (Note, that it is common to mistake these little noises or grunts as signs that your baby is waking up. Wait a moment to be sure he is waking up, before lifting him).

Halfway through the sleep cycle, babies pass from active to quiet sleep. Babies in quiet sleep breathe slower and more rhythmically, exhibit little movement, and are less likely to be awakened by noise and other types of disturbance. At the end of the sleep cycle, babies either wake up or the cycle starts over again. As babies mature, quiet sleep starts to separate into distinct NREM stages. Their sleep cycles become longer with proportionately less time spent in active or REM sleep.

Knowing more about sleep cycles helps you understand that no baby (or adult!) ever really sleeps through the night. Don't be frustrated when you hear other parents say that their three month old baby is already able to sleep in one long, continuous bout of sleep while you're still struggling to get more than two or three hours at a time. The babies who are "sleeping through the night" wake up several times but were probably able to fall back to sleep without waking their parents. It is also worth noting that while your sleep cycles are out of sync and your baby wakens you from a deep sleep you will feel particularly groggy and out of sorts. There really isn't much you can do about this other than understand that this period only lasts for a short time. On average it takes about six months for your baby to develop an adult sleep cycle.

In addition to having a different sleep cycle, during the first few months, your baby does not recognize the difference between night and day. This is not done as a means of torture! It's because at first, babies don't know that night time is for sleep and daytime is for being awake.

While inside the womb, your baby was tuned into your physiological cues. When you were active and going about your tasks during the day, his heart and respiratory rates increased. On the other hand, when you slowed down during the evenings, his heart and respiratory rates also decreased. These changes may be determined by a hormone called melatonin, which passes through the placenta and is likely to impact his internal clock. (There are some babies who become very active when their mother slows down to rest. This may be because they are receiving a greater share of oxygen at this time).

Once outside the womb, your baby no longer receives your hormones or is guided by your activity. He is focused only on survival so his sleep pattern will be influenced by how long it takes him to feed, digest, and become hungry once more. In addition, his instinct is to be more wakeful at night (and wake your more) as he is more vulnerable when you are asleep. During the day, when you are awake and vigilant, he feels safer so will generally sleep better. Again, keep in mind, at this early stage of his development, your baby is programmed for survival and has no knowledge that he is safe in your home at night.

A newborn's internal clock or circadian rhythm is far from developed when he is born but gradually this rhythm will mature over the first few months. Slowly patterns begin to emerge with daytime naps becoming increasingly shorter and night time sleeps longer.

Although confusing day and night is normal, it usually starts correcting itself when your baby is around three months old. At this point, his melatonin hormone production begins to resemble yours. By the time your baby is five or six months old, his internal clock will be fully developed, allowing him to sleep less during the day and longer at night. His stomach has grown considerably which also allows him to last longer between feeds.

Sleep summary - key points

During the first 3 months:

1. It is completely normal to wake frequently.
2. He is focussed solely on his own survival.
3. He needs to feed frequently as his tummy is tiny.
4. Day and night are irrelevant concepts.
5. Huge amount of development so needs to sleep a lot.
6. Often more wakeful at night when more vulnerable.
7. Sleep cycle out of sync with parents.

From 4 months to 6 months:

1. Tummy has grown so can take a bigger feed.
2. Sleeping longer at night with shorter day time naps.
3. Internal clock is more mature so beginning to understand day and night.
4. Sleep cycle becoming more like an adults.
5. Still needs a lot of sleep but sleep periods more consolidated.

Get to know your baby

With each passing moment and every interaction, you are getting to know your baby better. Understanding your baby's journey helps you to understand and respond to his needs more accurately and sensitively. Your knowledge about sleep patterns and sleep cycles will help you to manage your own expectations around normal baby sleep much more realistically.

Your baby has gone through a huge transition. During the early months, he is adjusting to the new and exciting world around him. He needs lots of sleep and must feed very regularly too. Frequent waking is normal. Your baby is not waking to annoy you and cannot 'manipulate' you at this early stage of development. He is unaware of the life of his care provider or their sleep cycle. He is only focused on his own survival and his sleep and waking patterns are designed perfectly to keep him alive and help him grow and develop.

Your baby is changing and maturing quickly. In a short space of time he will be sleeping longer and beginning to understand night and day. All babies are unique and will mature at different rates but by looking after yourself and staying calm, you can help your little one to happily settle in to his new life with minimum stress for you all.

Chapter 3: Your Parenting Style Makes a Difference

In the journey towards better sleep, understanding the parenting style you prefer will help you to determine what type of schedule that will work best for you, your baby and your family.

Parenting styles

The most popular ideas about parenting styles come from the work of Diane Baumrind. In the 1960s, Baumrind was interested in the different ways that parents attempted to control or socialise their children.

She proposed three distinct parenting styles:

Authoritarian parenting: This is a strict form of parenting that expects a child to adhere to rules set out by the parents. Authoritarian parents use punishments to control their child.

Permissive parenting: This is a very relaxed approach where parents are loving and affectionate but don't provide sufficient boundaries for their child or enforce rules. They are overly accepting of bad behaviour.

Authoritative parenting: This is a more balanced approach. Children are expected to meet behavioural standards but parenting is done in a warm and nurturing manner.

Uninvolved parenting, a fourth style, was added later in 1983 (Maccoby and Martin). This style is like permissive parenting as there is a failure to enforce standards. But unlike permissive parents, uninvolved parents are not nurturing and warm. They provide food and shelter, but not much else.

Children from authoritative families are usually well-behaved and successful at school. They tend to be emotionally healthy, resourceful, and socially-adept. Children from authoritarian families are more likely to show increased aggressive or defiant behavior over time. They are also more likely to suffer from anxiety, depression, or poor self-esteem. Children with permissive parents may be less likely to experience behavior or emotional problems but they may achieve less at school. Children from uninvolved families are the worst off in all respects. Most juvenile offenders have uninvolved parents (Steinberg 2001).

The above is only a brief summary and you may wish to explore the detail of different parenting styles further to determine what fits best for you. In addition, make sure you think about the style of all the adults involved in your baby's care to ensure a balance. How you were parented will also strongly influence the type of parent you want to be. Not everyone falls neatly in to a particular style but most find that they can relate to aspects of one or the other. Your cultural background also plays a part. The four styles mentioned above are based on observations of families in the US so are not necessarily appropriate for all cultures. Your style will also change and adapt over time as your baby grows and perhaps the size of your family changes.

Once you are comfortable with the type of parent you would like to be, this will help guide you day to day and plan for success. You may also wish to consider what type of daily schedule would work best for you.

Most parents are keen to introduce a schedule to achieve some order in their day and it can be helpful to understand the common methods used. Previous generations were encouraged to start routines very early in their baby's lives for fear of creating bad habits or spoiling them. We now know that during the first three months or fourth trimester, your priority should be to meet your baby's emotional and physiological needs first, before establishing a routine or schedule. From four months onwards, scheduling becomes more practical and effective.

Schedules basically fall in to three main categories. These are; parent-led, baby-led, and a combination schedule. What follows is an overview of each of the methods.

Parent-led schedules

A parent-led approach to scheduling involves creating a specific timetable for your baby's activities, including feeding, playtime, and sleeping. Timing is crucial in this method, and parent-led advocates, such as author Gary Ezzo and maternity nurse-turned-childcare expert Gina Ford, say it's important to stick to the schedule and to be extremely consistent in order to provide your baby the structure he needs to progress.

The basis for the parent-led method is the result of years of studying the natural rhythms of babies at various ages. According to proponents, this approach allows babies to fall into regular patterns more smoothly and helps babies sleep through the night sooner. In addition, this approach discourages nursing or rocking babies to sleep since babies need to learn to fall asleep on their own.

Feeding is also very structured under parent-led schedules, with advocates warning against breastfeeding on demand because according to them, it's likely that new parents would consider almost every cry of their baby as a sign of hunger, instead of looking for other causes first. This could result in a tiring routine of perpetual feedings that last well beyond the baby's newborn months. The American Academy of Pediatrics (AAP), disagrees with this kind of structured feeding. According to the AAP, "the best feeding schedules are ones babies design themselves." Therefore, they recommend feeding babies on demand, particularly when they exhibit hunger signs like heightened activity or alertness, mouthing, or rooting.

Starting early is key when establishing parent-led schedules and this often means training a very young baby. Meals, playtimes, naps, and other activities must happen at a predetermined time. As the baby gets older, the schedule changes but the activities and when they should take place are still clearly established.

When following this approach with a newborn, it is important for your baby to be healthy and he should have weighed at least six pounds at birth since in some schedules, the baby needs to go three hours between feeds. This rigid quality of the parent-led method is one of its biggest disadvantages since it can keep parents from focusing on the well-being of their babies in order to stick to the schedule.

A parent-led schedule does provide order and pattern to a day that can make life easier for parents. This method is not beneficial to babies who need responsive parenting in the early months. (It can work well with toddlers who feel secure with a routine.) However, parents who have been successful with this method reported their babies slept through the night at an earlier age. This aspect makes the approach appealing to new parents with specific needs such as returning to work soon after birth.

Baby-led schedules

In contrast to parent-led schedules, baby-led schedules are highly flexible routines that follow your baby's cues to decide what he wants to do next. While this type of schedule doesn't seem like a schedule at all, babies eventually form their own regular patterns after a few weeks. However, the schedule may vary from one day to the next, depending on the signals your baby gives you. For instance, he may nap at ten a.m. one day and at twelve thirty p.m. the next.

The idea behind the baby-led schedule is that each child is unique so a set method that works for one may not work for another. This approach was recommended by Benjamin Spock, a famed paediatrician, who informed parents that babies didn't have to follow a specified feeding and sleep schedule because they have their own distinct personalities and needs. As a result, Dr Spock encouraged mothers to feed on demand, or whenever their baby showed signs of hunger.

If you don't mind changing your daily routine to accommodate your baby, this parenting style could work well for you. Likewise, if your baby has no consistent pattern in his routine, he could thrive with this approach. To establish a baby-led schedule, you need to first make sure that your baby's basic needs for food, interaction, and sleep are met. Although your days may vary, these elements have to be met consistently. Moreover, you need to spend plenty of time with and be attentive to your baby in order to learn his signs for when he is hungry or sleepy.

Following the baby's lead when it comes to bedtime is particularly helpful since sleep is not something you can force your child to do. Dr William Sears, a paediatrician and his wife, Martha, a registered nurse, advocate "night time parenting," which involves feeding, rocking, cuddling, and other ways to get your baby to sleep. For the Sears', getting your baby to sleep through the night is not as important as helping your child develop a healthy sleep attitude.

Proponents of the baby-led approach believe that this schedule type promotes a closer relationship between you and your baby. This ultimately leads to a happier child. It also supports what we know about our baby's needs during the fourth trimester. This can make the baby led approach more relaxing as you tend to 'go with the flow' rather than fighting against nature.

You can also enjoy a certain amount of freedom since you don't need to follow a rigid set of rules about when your baby should feed, play, or sleep. Furthermore, this type of schedule can make your baby more adaptable to schedule changes, which has been the experience of some parents who have been successful with the baby-led routine.

The baby-led approach is not for everyone, especially if you're a working parent. It can be too exhausting since you always have to be there to comfort your child in order for him to fall asleep. In addition, your baby could become very dependent on you to read his cues and it may be difficult or impossible to leave him with another caregiver.

Combination schedules

A mix of the parent-led and baby-led routines, the combination approach necessitates setting a program for when your baby will eat, sleep, play, and so on. In general, you stick to a similar routine every day, which makes it different than some baby-led schedules. But, unlike parent-led routines, you enjoy more flexibility and take signals from your baby on what to do next. For instance, lunch can be pushed back if a trip out takes longer than anticipated, or a nap can be delayed if your baby doesn't seem tired yet.

The combination approach to scheduling offers the consistency that both you and your child needs without having to adhere to a strict routine. Paediatrician Marc Weissbluth is the author of Healthy Sleep Habits, Healthy Child, a book which offers parents general sleep schedules to promote healthy sleep patterns. The theoretical basis for Dr Weissbluth's method is when your baby is well-rested, other activities in the day all fall into place. While taking cues from your child is necessary to know when to get your baby to sleep, it shouldn't stop you from employing other means, such as soothing your baby or letting him skip an afternoon nap as long as these don't happen often.

If you appreciate both structure and flexibility when deciding on your baby's schedule, the combination method is for you. You and your baby have a dependable routine to rely on, but you won't be thrown if changes on a particular day require a shift in your schedule. This method is also ideal if your baby loves predictability, but doesn't get fussy if nap times get pushed back.

Make the right choice for you

Babies don't come with instruction books and it's up to parents to determine the best way to raise their child. Having an awareness of different styles of parenting and the influence they have on a developing baby is important, not just for yourself but for all those involved with your baby's care. Understanding your own style will help you develop in to the parent you want to be rather than the parent your children make you. Authoritative parenting is considered to produce the most well-balanced children but this does not work in all cultures and all families. Uninvolved parenting should be avoided as the outcomes for children with this type parenting are not good.

Deciding on the type of daily routine or schedule that you prefer will be influenced by your parenting style. Other factors such as whether you are working or caring for other children will also help determine which choice is best for you. The most important thing is that it's your decision and is one that you feel happy and comfortable with. Don't feel pressurised in to behaviour that is fashionable or someone else's view. Use your own common sense and be guided by what feels best for you and your baby.

My experience

The strongest influence on my early parenting days was how I was parented myself. I had quite strong views on the things that I felt my parents had done well and also the things that I wasn't so keen on. Some aspects were also influenced by new research, fashion, my peers and a change in generations. As my family grew, I also grew in confidence and gradually developed my own parenting style which I still use today. Authoritative parenting works best for me although there have been times over the years that I have briefly stepped in to authoritarian parenting (for example during toddler and teenage tantrums!) On the whole I love being a parent and have made the most of every stage.

With respect to schedules, I had none for about the first six weeks of my first born's life! Baby led would most closely describe our routine. As we have generous maternity leave in the UK I was lucky to be off work for many months and could gradually develop a relaxed combination schedule over time. This worked well for us both as it allowed me to get to know him and what was best for his personality.

Chapter 4: Creating a Great and Safe Sleep Environment

Key to your baby sleeping well is a great sleep environment which encourages sound slumber with minimum disturbance. This is relatively easy to achieve but it is important to know how to do this safely. Recommended baby sleep guidelines are described below on how to prepare your little one's sleep setup safely. It is also useful to think about what the perfect sleep setup is from you baby's perspective. Understanding your baby's reality will help you to manage your own expectations.

Note: If your baby has passed the fourth trimester, use this chapter to review your existing sleep set up. See if there are improvements you can make to your sleep environment to encourage better sleep.

Your baby's perfect place to sleep

1. Safely in the arms of someone calm and loving (or in very close proximity to them).

2. A source of food readily available (breast milk is perfect).

Remember – your baby's key objective is about survival. Biologically he has not evolved much in the last few thousand years. In his world, his best chance of survival is to be in constant contact with his main care provider.

Many babies around the world are still cared for in this way. However, for parents in Western cultures, this type of care is rarely practical beyond the early days and weeks after birth. For that reason, where and how your baby sleeps is very important.

The purpose of this chapter is to guide you on how to make informed decisions around your baby's sleep setup and environment – whatever part of the world you are from.

Best practice for safe baby sleep

Since the beginning of time, parents have instinctively tended to their babies and known how best to keep them safe and cared for. These basic parenting instincts and 'gut feelings' are still very important today. You know your baby better than anyone else and your baby will feel most safe and secure with you. Research has highlighted some important information with regards to your baby's safety, particularly safe baby sleep. Much of our knowledge has been gained from research into Sudden Infant Death Syndrome. (This research resulted in the 'Back to Sleep' Campaign in the UK, which reduced the incidence by fifty percent).

What is Sudden Infant Death Syndrome?

Sometimes called cot death or crib death, sudden infant death syndrome (SIDS) is the abrupt and unexpected death of a baby within its first year of life. Using the definition 'cot' or 'crib' death can be misleading as SIDS can happen during the day or night and does not have to be in a crib or cot. It can happen in a car seat, bouncy chair or even in the arms of a caregiver.

Although it was once thought that the victims were healthy infants that were randomly affected, it is now believed that while SIDS babies seemed perfectly healthy on the outside, in some cases they did have underlying problems that made them more susceptible to sudden death.

One of the theories about babies who suffered from SIDS is that they may have lower levels of serotonin in their brain. Serotonin is the chemical that controls breathing and heart rate during sleep. Having low levels of serotonin makes it more difficult for babies to wake up or rouse themselves from a deep sleep.

It is important to state that the risk of SIDS happening is very low. However, while it can be hard to determine whether a baby is at risk, there is an increased risk among:

1. Premature babies
2. Low birth weight babies
3. Infants who are exposed to cigarette smoke

Additionally, three in every five SIDS victims are boys, and African American as well as Native American infants are two to three times more predisposed to the syndrome.

Ways to reduce the risk of SIDS

There has been considerable research in to the cause of SIDS over recent decades resulting in guidelines and safe sleeping advice produced by many professional bodies and global organisations such as Unicef, The American Academy of Paediatrics and the National Institute of Clinical Excellence (NICE) in the UK. They all agree on the key aspects of how to reduce the risk of SIDS and these are listed below.

Note however, although the guidelines advise how to reduce the risk of SIDS, this should not lull you into a false sense of security. As a parent to a newborn it's best to be very vigilant. Although some of the advice seems more applicable to babies during the fourth trimester period, much of the advice is equally as appropriate for older babies. Just adapt accordingly. For example, once your baby is able to roll and move about, you will no longer be able to keep him sleeping on his back. Don't worry. This is fine and a normal aspect of his development.

1. **Place your baby on his back:** When putting your baby down to sleep, always place him on his back. This position increases the baby's access to fresh air and reduces the likelihood of overheating. (Some infants sleep better and deeper on their stomachs but this position increases the risk of SIDS. Placing him on his side is also discouraged as he may roll onto his stomach).

2. **Breastfeed your baby:** Numerous studies have supported the protective effects of breastfeeding with one study concluding that it can reduce the risk of SIDS by up to half. Even a brief period of breastfeeding can be protective for your baby but ideally he should be fed for his first 6 months to gain the maximum benefit.

3. **Keep your baby away from cigarette smoke:** Smoking greatly increases the risk of SIDS and your baby can be affected by either you or your partner smoking. Keep your baby's environment smoke free at home and when you are out and about.

4. **Room share for at least your baby's first six months:** The safest place for your baby to sleep is in a cot or crib in the same room as you during the night (and for day sleeping). The risk of SIDS is reduced when your baby sleeps in the same room as you but in his own cot rather than in your bed with you.

5. **Give your child a pacifier (or dummy):** Sucking on a pacifier has been shown to lower the risk of SIDS. If you're breastfeeding, wait for your baby to become established with his feeds before offering a pacifier. Don't force your baby if he doesn't want it and don't pop the pacifier back in if it drops out while he's asleep.

6. **Avoid your baby overheating:** Young babies are unable to control their body temperature so make sure that the room is neither too hot nor too cold for your little one. Overheating can increase the risk of SIDS so always ensure your baby is dressed appropriately. While there is no exact temperature specified, experts recommend keeping the room temperature between sixty five – seventy two Farenheight or sixteen - twenty Centigrade. It's a good idea to invest in a room thermometer so you'll always know the temperature of your room. Don't let this become a source of anxiety though. Use your common sense if necessary just as our parents and ancestors did before the invention of thermometers. If it's warm, take a layer of clothing or a blanket off your baby. Do the reverse if it's cooler. You can test if he is too hot by laying your hand on his back or stomach to feel if he is hot or clammy. (Hands and feet are naturally cooler so don't rely on their temperature).

7. **Know how to perform baby CPR:** Whether you end up having to or not, it's essential to know how you can resuscitate your child if he stops breathing. If nothing else, having this skill can help you sleep better at night.

Other sleep safety tips

Cribs and Cots: Whether you're buying a new crib or getting a hand-me-down, make sure it meets the safety standard set by your country such as the Consumer Product Safety Commission (CPSC) or the Juvenile Products Manufacturers Association (JPMA) in the US or the British Safety Standard in the UK. If assembling the crib yourself, check the manual to ensure that you have all the right pieces and it is correctly assembled.

You shouldn't use the crib if any of the following apply:

- the sides go down
- there are design cut outs in the headboard or footboard (often found in older cribs and cots)
- you can fit a drinks can between the slats of the crib
- the corner posts stick up (they should be flush with the sides)

To avoid trapping or strangling, place the crib away from wall-mounted decorations, windows, blinds, and draperies. Avoid hanging anything on or over the crib on a string or cord.

Mattress and bedding: A firm, flat mattress which has a waterproof cover is best. It should fit snugly in to the cot or crib with no gaps. You should also use a sheet that fits the mattress tightly. Bedding should be firmly tucked in and cover no higher than your baby's shoulders. Baby sleeping bags or sleeper sacks work well as long as you choose the correct warmth level for the season and your home/room temperature. There are many other sleep products available to buy such as in-bed sleep aids. These can be very expensive and there is currently no research evidence to confirm or deny how good they are.

Keep an uncluttered crib: Avoid crib bumpers, pillows, toys, and other objects as these all increase the risk of SIDS. Keep your baby's sleep space clear to avoid any accidents.

Clothing: When dressing your baby for sleep, choose clothes made of material and thickness that is appropriate for the season. Remove strings or ties that could wrap around little fingers. If it's cold, add another lightweight blanket or dress your baby in a sleeper sack. His head should always be uncovered to prevent overheating. Blankets should be tucked securely into the foot of the bed and with just enough length to cover your baby up to his shoulders.

Creating a great sleep environment

So far, we have only considered how to keep your baby safe during sleep times but there are other things you should think about to promote better sleep. In reality, babies will always sleep when they need to and have done so in many environments for thousands of years without black out blinds or white noise machines. However, every baby is different and just like adults, all have preferences on how they like to sleep. Many parents swear by the following tips but don't rush out and buy lots of new stuff. Try one idea at a time for a minimum of a week. See if it helps before considering if there is a need to try the next idea.

Lighting: Because the internal clock of a newborn is not yet developed, it's best to keep daytime bright and night time dark to help your little one distinguish between day and night. Whether your baby sleeps in the same room as you do or in his own room, the room should be dark when it's time for bed to encourage his body to produce the sleep hormone melatonin.

Make sure that any lights in the bedroom are not too bright. If you need to get up in the middle of the night, have a faint light that emits a natural red or yellow glow. You and your baby shouldn't be exposed to televisions, smartphones, and similar gadgets at least ninety minutes before bed because these devices emit blue light, which actually inhibit the release of melatonin. Consider using blackout curtains if there are artificial light sources outside the house, like a streetlamp.

Noise: While keeping the room dark at night is helpful, blocking out noise completely is not. From the time he was inside the womb, your baby has been exposed to all sorts of noise from your beating heart to the sound of your voice. Keeping the room totally devoid of any sound could actually keep your baby from getting a good night's sleep. Many parents swear by a white noise machine, which produces soothing noises, such as rain falling. Playing white noise could be helpful if you live in a noisy part of a city or town.

Keep the room clutter-free: Apart from removing possible distractions for your baby, keeping the room organized and free from clutter makes it a calming space for both you and your child. In addition, keeping the room orderly prevents you from accidentally stepping or slipping on a toy or another object that could create noise that will wake your baby or lead to you injuring yourself. This is particularly important at night when lights are low and you are tired and sleepy.

Keep room décor simple. At first babies can only see black and white but gradually, as their eyesight develops, they are drawn to bright colours. Too much colour can over stimulate a young baby and this could keep them from sound sleep. Likewise, mobiles can be quite distracting and even overwhelming when they are tired so avoid these for best results.

Smell: The smell of the room or even your baby's clothing and bedding could affect the quality of his sleep. If your room or your baby's was recently painted, make sure to air it out. The same goes for any of the furniture. As for the clothing, choose a detergent that has a very mild scent or even one without any scent at all. A familiar smell can help settle your baby too. Try laying a blanket with your scent on it next to him. This can be very comforting.

Should I bed share?

Bed sharing is an important concept to understand as, at one time or another, most babies spend time sharing a bed with their parents – whether this was planned or not. Planned bed sharing is much safer than letting it happen accidentally therefore, plan to do it safely. The Infant Sleep Information Service provides great advice www.isisonline.co.uk.

In many parts of the world, such as Asia, Africa, Southern Europe, as well as Central and South America, bed sharing is a natural part of the daily life of parents. In some countries where bed sharing is the normal practice, sudden infant death syndrome is virtually unheard of and they have no specific word in their language to describe this condition. In the US and the UK particularly, the issue of bed sharing continues to divide the population about its safety and the other benefits parents and children can get out of it.

In the interest of clarity for this book, bed sharing means the parent or parents sleeping in the same bed as the baby. Sometimes the term 'co-sleeping' is used to describe the same thing but this could also refer to the parent sleeping in the bed while the baby sleeps in a co-sleeper, a type of crib or attachment that can be adjusted to the height of the bed. As we have read from the previous section on Sudden Infant Death Syndrome, the recommendation is to share a room with your baby for the first six months, and even up to a year. The guidelines however discourage bed-sharing due to its potential dangers to a young baby.

Whether intending to bed share or not, it is important to understand the advantages and disadvantages. This is because, often through sheer exhaustion, some parents take their baby into bed with them as it seems like the only way to get some sleep. If you need help deciding whether this would work for you and your infant, consider the following pros and cons of bed sharing as reported by researchers and parents.

Advantages of sharing a bed with your baby

Bed sharing promotes breastfeeding: Bed sharing babies are more likely to be breastfed, especially at night since the mother and child are in close proximity. During the first few weeks of your baby's life, breastfeeding can be a challenge if your baby sleeps in another room and you have to get up several times during the night for feeding. Because bed sharing makes breastfeeding so much more convenient, most mothers breastfeed longer.

Increased night time breastfeeding also provides a number of benefits, including the promotion of the baby's growth and good sleep since breast milk produced at night contains more growth hormone as well as melatonin. As a result, babies who are breastfed gain weight more quickly and are more resistant to childhood illnesses and infections. Furthermore, mothers benefit from frequent night time breastfeeding because the longer they breastfeed, the lower their risk of developing breast, uterine, and cervical cancer.

Bed sharing reduces the risk of SIDS: We know that sharing a room with your new born reduces the risk of SIDS especially during the first six months but does sharing the same bed have the same effect? Some studies have shown that it can promote the synchronization of the mother's and baby's breathing and heart rates. This means that the mother is alerted to any irregular changes in her baby's breathing pattern, or the baby "remembers" to breathe in response to the mother's breathing. It is interesting to note that in Japan, which has the lowest rates of SIDS in the world, bed-sharing and breastfeeding (in the absence of maternal smoking) is the typical cultural practice.

Your baby feels safe: Hearing and feeling the rhythmic sound of your breathing and warmth naturally calms your baby, which is why a baby cries less when its mother is close by.

Bed sharing fosters closeness between the parent and child: Although researchers haven't found conclusive evidence to support the theory that bed sharing promotes strong bonds between mother and child, many parents still believe being close to each other is comforting to both. The close proximity also allows you to check on your baby and to touch and soothe him easily.

It can help you get more sleep: For parents, one of the biggest benefits you can get from bed sharing is that it allows you to get more snooze time. In fact, the main reason why most mothers bed share is to breastfeed while still having time to sleep. Neither you or your baby need to be fully awake during feeding so going back to sleep is easier. While you may have a lighter sleep, experts say that this type of sleep is better than the sleep you get when you have to get up at night to breastfeed or bottle feed a child in a different room.

Disadvantages of sharing a bed with your baby

Bed-sharing is considered unsafe by the American Academy of Paediatrics: When a young baby shares a bed with his parents, he could be suffocated by the pillows or sheets. It's also possible for either parent to roll on top of the baby, or for the baby to be caught in the space between the bed and the mattress. In addition, a bed sharing baby who is already able to crawl can fall off the bed, although incidences of this are very low.

It affects the quality of sleep: Some parents find it difficult to fully relax and sleep for fear of rolling onto and suffocating their baby. The baby could also have difficulty sleeping soundly due to his parents' movements as well as snoring.

It interferes with the intimacy between the parents: Most parents find it difficult to be intimate if their baby is in bed with them. They either have to move to a different room or forego intimacy until the baby can sleep in his own bed.

It could promote too much dependence: Babies need to learn to fall asleep on their own. Unfortunately, bed sharing could make the process take longer and could make your baby too dependent on you during bedtime, making it harder to sleep on his own in the future.

Bed sharing safety advice

Bed sharing should be avoided if either you or your partner; are smokers or use e-cigarettes (even if you never smoke in bed or at home), have been drinking alcohol, or have taken any medications or drugs that could cause drowsiness. You should also avoid bed sharing if your baby is premature (born earlier than 37 weeks), or had a low birth weight (less than 5.5 lbs). Also, don't sleep with your baby on a sofa or a make-shift bed. This is extremely unsafe and can cause the death of a baby. Most sofas have cushions and corners that can trap your baby and smother him. If you have long hair, make sure you keep it tied. Take off jewellery before going to bed to avoid tiny fingers getting trapped or swallowing accidents.

Keep your sleep environment safe and simple

Keeping your baby safe during sleep times is of the utmost importance. By following the safe sleep guidelines described in this chapter, you can reduce the risk of Sudden Infant Death Syndrome significantly. If you intend to bed share with your baby, make sure you understand the advice on how to do this safely before you take your baby into bed with you. Your baby's needs are simple when it comes to sleep requirements so resist the temptation to invest in lots of sleep enhancing items until you are sure you need them as this can be money wasted. Now that you've got your sleep environment sorted, read on to the next chapter to find out how to settle your baby down to sleep successfully.

Chapter 5: Preparing your Baby for Sleep

Although all babies are different and all families are different, there are some key principles which will help you prepare your baby for sleep. If you follow these principles (and with a little perseverance), you will achieve success.

If your baby is in the fourth trimester (or newborn phase), the first step is to take the time to learn when he is sleepy. You do this by baby watching. Baby watching involves spending lots of time holding and looking at your infant. Although at first it is difficult to distinguish between his different cries, facial expressions or movements, through observation, you will gradually begin to make sense of what he is telling you. This will allow you to respond better to his needs with the result that there is less distress for both you and your baby. It's also a lovely way to get to know him really well, deepen your bond and feel very connected. When it comes to tiredness, he will have his own way to show you that he needs to sleep. It is up to you and his other carers to learn these signals and act accordingly.

If your baby is passed the fourth trimester (or newborn stage), the techniques used to help settle him down for sleep such as introducing a sleep time routine, are described later in this chapter. You may still find it a useful reminder to read the whole chapter to understand your baby's journey so far and the role you have played in it.

Learning to soothe your baby

Before your baby can fall asleep, he needs to feel relaxed and safe. Achieving this should be your number one aim, whatever his age or stage. Creating an environment that is calm and peaceful is essential. If your baby is very overstimulated or crying and distressed, you will need to help him calm down before beginning your sleep time preparation. To do this, firstly check how calm you are feeling. If you are stressed out, your baby will pick up these signals. If you are feeling calm, holding and cuddling your baby will help him activate the calming part of his brain. Warmth also helps relaxation so snuggle him up in a warm blanket while you cuddle him. Alternatively try a warm bath or a lovely relaxing massage (for your baby, not for you unfortunately!) which will also help him settle down. Movements such as rocking and swaying, can also be very soothing. If these techniques don't work, consider some of the reasons below.

Twelve reasons why your baby may be crying

Crying is one way your baby communicates his needs. If you are not able to settle him, take a quick look at this list and see if you have missed anything.

1. **Hungry:** As a parent, one of the first things you check when your baby cries is whether he is hungry. However, when a baby cries because of hunger it means you've missed his initial hunger cues. Avoid the crying stage by watching out for fussing, lip smacking, fist/finger sucking, and rooting. Rooting is a reflex of newborns where they turn their head toward your hand when you touch their cheek. They often open their mouths in search of a nipple or breast. Offer milk to your baby once he exhibits these behaviours.
2. **Wind:** Newborns sometimes cry after a feed because they need to burp. While burping is not mandatory, some parents make it a point to try to burp their baby after every feed. If back rubbing and patting don't work,

try putting your baby on his tummy over your knee and gently massage his back.

3. **Diaper or nappy change:** Some babies can tolerate a dirty diaper longer than others but it's essential to check your baby every now and then (when he is awake) to prevent irritation.

4. **Overtired:** Overtired babies have a harder time falling asleep so avoid the crying stage related to tiredness by observing and acting on your baby's sleep cues.

5. **Needs to be close to you:** Babies crave touch. They also like smelling their mother and fathers unique scent, or listening to their parents' voices. Carrying your baby is important during the first few months since he longs for the snug and safe environment inside your womb. Baby wearing is a great way to hold your baby close while you go about your day.

6. **Too hot or cold:** Young babies are not able to regulate their own temperature. Check he is not too hot by placing your hand on his tummy or back. If he feels hot or clammy, remove a layer of clothing. Make sure your baby isn't too cold either as this might also make him cry - more so than if he were too warm. **Note:** Remember to loosen clothing and take off hats and gloves when moving inside while shopping during colder weather. It's easy to forget and your baby can quickly overheat.

7. **Over stimulated:** Compared to the snug and relatively quiet conditions inside the womb, the outside world can be an overwhelming place for a baby. If you think your baby is getting too much stimulation, move him to somewhere quiet and calm with less sensory input.

8. **Under stimulated:** Some babies are naturally outgoing and curious about the world so they get fussy when they don't get much stimulation. Taking walks outside,

visiting friends or relatives, driving around the neighbourhood, or just wearing your baby in a carrier while you do household chores or run errands can be entertaining for your little one.

9. **Teething:** A baby's first tooth usually appears between four and seven months, but this can happen earlier. While some can tolerate the pain more than others, an emerging tooth can still cause a degree of discomfort. You can check if your baby is crying because of teething by running your finger along his gums to feel for little teeth coming through. You can try applying a teething gel, but if you're concerned about the possible side effects, give your baby a silicone teether that has been cooled in the fridge instead.

10. **Not feeling well:** It can be very worrying if you suspect your baby is unwell. If you are a first time parent, you may feel you don't want to keep calling your Doctor as you believe you should be able to tell if you baby is ill or not. This is not the case. Small babies can become unwell quickly so always call your Doctor for advice if you are concerned.

11. **Gassy or colicky:** If your baby cries or fusses after feeding, he may be suffering from gas. If burping doesn't work, place the baby on his back and try bicycling his legs gently until the gas passes. You can also talk to your doctor or breastfeeding counsellor to rule out feeding issues.

12. **Fingers or toes are wrapped in a hair tourniquet:** This is when a piece of hair is wrapped tightly around a finger or any other body part, cutting off circulation. This happens more often than you think, which is why it is one of the first things doctors check when a baby seems to be crying "for no reason." If you have a baby boy, check that nothing is wrapped around his penis as

hair, loose threads, or fibres can find their way inside the nappy.

Recreating the womb can help young babies

For difficult to settle babies, recreating the environment in the womb might be more effective in helping them fall asleep. Here are some things you can try.

Movement: Babies are used to being jostled and swayed inside the womb, which is why movement often calms an overtired or unsettled infant. Baby swings, baby hammocks, and rocking bassinets are great for this purpose. You could also try baby wearing if being close to you is what relaxes your little one. Once your baby is drowsy, transition to cuddling so he will get used to sleeping without movement. Eventually, you can place him in his bed, drowsy but still awake, after just a couple of minutes of cuddling.

Darkness: Keeping the room where your baby sleeps in complete darkness is not only calming for your baby at bedtime, it also blocks out visual distractions. If your baby is overstimulated at bedtime and has trouble falling asleep or staying asleep, try using blackout curtains.

Sound: Your baby was exposed to plenty of sounds inside the womb so he might be uncomfortable in a room where there is absolutely no noise. Of course, he would also have difficulty sleeping if the opposite were true. In any case, a white noise machine that plays rain sounds, waves, or washing machine and vacuuming sounds, can be helpful in providing the necessary noise and drowning out the others. Shushing sounds can also be very calming

Hard to settle babies

Some babies just seem to cry a lot and are difficult to settle. Research shows that this can happen for many different reasons. These include reasons such as; the baby experienced a difficult birth, the baby has health issues or the pregnancy was stressful. (Babies receive stress hormones through the placenta from their mother. This can result in fussier babies). Parental perception also plays a part. Depending on expectations, attitudes to crying vary from parent to parent. One family may consider the amount of crying normal while another considers it excessive even when the baby is actually crying for the same amount of time. More recent research suggests that for many babies, prolonged, unexplained crying is purely a developmental stage and these babies are perfectly healthy and normal. For further information on this, visit www.purplecrying.info.

Whatever the reason, having a crying baby who you are unable to comfort can be very distressing for parents. If you feel you have tried everything, it is important to get your baby checked out by a medical professional to ensure there are no health reasons. Seeking support from other parents in similar situations can also be helpful and reduce feelings of isolation.

Get to know your baby's sleep 'cues'

Understanding your baby's sleep cues will go a long way in helping your baby to have a sound sleep. Eye-rubbing, yawning, and turning away are just some of the things most babies do when they're tired and want to sleep. However, every child has different sleep cues so it's important to know the signs that mean your baby is ready for bed. Once you see these cues, it's time to respond appropriately and allow your baby to go to sleep. If you don't act on them right away or you missed the signs, it can lead your baby to become over tired, which makes it that much harder to get him settled.

Common baby sleep cues

Turning away: Babies can become overstimulated very easily. Breaking eye contact is a sign that he is feeling overwhelmed, and wants less stimulation. Turning away may be accompanied by crying or playing with his fingers or toes. When this happens, respect your child's need for a break. Wait for him to look at you again instead of trying to move into his line of sight.

Sucking on fingers or thumb: Sucking is a way that your baby uses to comfort and calm himself.

Drawing arms and legs in towards his body: This can also be a sign that your baby is feeling overstimulated. Pulling in his limbs helps to calm his inner distress systems.

Frowning: One of the earliest signs of sleepiness, frowning is your baby's way of showing that he is not comfortable about something, which is often the case when he is tired. This may be accompanied by eye-rubbing.

Eye-rubbing: Sleepiness often comes with an itchy feeling in the eyes that causes babies to rub them.

Yawning: Your baby's yawns may not be noticeable at first, but they are a good indicator that he is sleepy. If you've missed the first few yawns, he would probably yawn more loudly, much like an adult would.

Whining: When your baby reaches the point of being extremely uncomfortable or overly tired, he may start whining. If you keep ignoring this, the whining will progress into a full-fledged cry.

Through baby watching, you will get to know your baby better and begin to learn all the different things he is communicating to you. Use his sleep cues to help you work out when it is bed or nap time.

Once you have soothed your baby and established that he is sleepy, the next step is to begin your sleep time preparation.

During the first few months, this will simply consist of laying your baby down to sleep, following the safe sleep guidelines, in your chosen place. This sleep place may be different during the day and at night and indeed, this can help the process of distinguishing between these two times. It is unlikely you will have much of a routine during the first three months. If you can, keep this time flexible and responsive to your baby's needs and it will be much more relaxing for you all.

If your baby is beyond this stage, you are ready to introduce a routine to suit the time of day. The night time or longest sleep time routine usually becomes established with day time routines shorter and more flexible.

Introducing a sleep time routine

There are no right or wrong routines for preparing your baby for sleep as long as the routine helps him calm down, relax and feel that he is safe to go to sleep. Equally though, your baby needs to fit in to your family life. Many things such as other siblings, being a single parent, work, or your own health will dictate the amount of time and how much effort you are able to spend on this activity. Keep things simple and flexible. This allows space for your different energy levels, inevitable interruptions and ups and downs of everyday life. Although initially it may be difficult to achieve a consistent routine, most parents find it helpful to begin a gentle sleep routine with their baby, even when he is only a few months old. It can give a small sense of structure to a day that can sometimes feel a little out of control. The other benefit is that babies like routines. It helps them to make sense of their day and when a routine is established, they understand what is likely to happen next. If you already have children, it is often easier to 'slot' the new arrival in to his sibling's routine.

For most parents, the evening bed time routine becomes the most established routine. Getting your baby settled at night is top priority in order for everyone to get some sleep. This night routine is also the one that will carry on through your child's life until they are able to put themselves to bed on their own. Although you will still be looking out for sleep cues during the day, your baby's nap time routine will likely be shorter. As your child grows, nap times reduce and as their night sleep gets longer, naps eventually disappear. We will therefore focus on bed time routines but these ideas can be used at any time of the day. Do what works for you and your family.

Establishing a bed time routine

Think about what time you would like your baby to go to bed and work back from there. Sometimes a gentle bedtime routine can start an hour or two before the actual bedtime and may include activities that are not directly related to the idea of going to bed. For instance, turning the TV off and other devices two hours before bed. Putting your phone on silent. Encourage other family members to speak softly, especially before taking your baby to the bedroom or nursery. Some older babies don't like the feeling of missing out on anything exciting so if you take your baby out of a quiet environment to another quiet environment, he wouldn't mind the change so much.

Top tip: Make sure you have your sleep set up ready before you begin your routine to avoid disruption or stress. Always have a change of bedding available in case of last minute accidents with milk or nappy contents!

Gentle bedtime routine ideas

- **Bath:** Not only is the warm water soothing to babies, bath time is also a great opportunity for you to talk and interact with your baby even if he's too young to understand. You can continue the tradition as he grows older so this becomes a special time for you to have relaxing conversations about anything under the sun. However, not all babies love baths. If your little one gets too excited about bathing (or he doesn't enjoy it at all), you might want to wait until he is older before making this a part of your bedtime routine.
- **Massage:** Giving a massage is one of the best ways to help your baby to relax before bedtime. It also provides a bonding opportunity for the baby and massager. There are classes which teach you how to give your baby a massage. They can be very relaxing for you too.
- **Reading:** There is no such thing as being too early when it comes to instilling a child's love for books

and reading, so make reading bedtime stories part of your ritual. Even if your baby doesn't understand the words yet, he will love listening to the sound of your voice. Why not read this book out loud to him? ▯

- **Lullaby:** Many lullabies are perfect for bedtime and singing a few of these can help your little one easily drift off to dreamland. Don't worry if singing is not your best attribute, you baby will still enjoy your calm, soothing voice.
- **Music:** While performing your bedtime rituals, play classical music, nursery rhymes, or any other type of music that your baby likes. If it's you who needs to relax, play some chill out or wind down music in the background. It can also help drown out noise that could otherwise be distracting.

Normally the bedtime routine will include a last feed. At which point you feed your baby during the routine is up to you. Most people choose to do this last as, especially for younger babies, they quite often fall asleep during feeding. Don't worry if this happens. Many parents worry about their baby becoming too dependent on the breast or bottle to fall asleep. Remember that sleeping in your arms with food on tap is your baby's idea of heaven. Being able to do this is an important part of his development and eventually he will grow out of it. It is a very special time which will pass in the blink of an eye so when possible, try to enjoy the moment. When you are ready to move him to the place where he sleeps, lay him gently in his bed following the safe sleep guidelines. It's sensible to give the last feed very close to where your baby sleeps to avoid unnecessary movement. Don't worry either about burping or winding in this situation. Your baby will wake up and let you know if he has wind.

For older babies or those who don't fall asleep when feeding, cuddle him until he becomes drowsy. If you've read his cues correctly and timed the ritual just so, this won't take too long. Next, put your baby on his back in the cot awake. If he is calm, you can start putting him down drowsy but still awake. Comfort him with gentle patting and shushing sounds if needed. When he is almost asleep, slowly move away from the crib. If your baby cries, wait a moment to see if he settles himself. (Some babies need a little cry before nodding off). If he continues to cry, return to his bed and reassure him with your voice and by stroking and patting him. Repeat this pattern for a few minutes until he is settled. Avoid letting him cry for a prolonged period as he will then take longer to settle down again.

Night waking is normal

As previously explained, it is perfectly normal for young babies to wake up regularly during the night to feed. As they get older, they begin to sleep longer between feeds. The time when this happens varies enormously from baby to baby and even those who seemed to sleep well from an early age can revert to waking again when they are older. Add to this the fact that a baby's sleep cycle is shorter than adults so they are naturally waking up more. The result is that babies are actually terrible sleepers! Acceptance of this fact and knowing that this stage will not last forever, can help you cope. Once your baby has passed the newborn stage, try waiting before you go to him when he wakes up. Wait for a minute or two to see if he can settle himself back to sleep. You can also make shushing sounds from the bed if he is sleeping close by to see if that is enough to comfort him. If you do need to feed or change him, keep lights very low, avoid eye contact and talking. Ensure that conditions are very different from when he wakes from a daytime nap when you can greet him with a big smile and lots of energy.

Create a routine that you enjoy

For normal healthy babies, calm, consistent treatment from loving and sensitive parents or carers who respond to their sleep cues will result in relaxed bed times with babies going to sleep without a fuss. Use baby watching to learn the signs that he is sleepy. This will avoid him becoming overstimulated or overtired. It is essential that both you and your baby are calm before sleep will be achieved.

For older babies, a sleep time routine can be an enjoyable part of the day. Once you find a routine that works, apply the same steps at roughly the same time and gradually your baby will learn that this means it is time for sleeping. And finally, develop a routine that makes you happy. You need to be able to enjoy these rituals as they will become an important part of your day to day life. They can also create a very special time for your baby too both now and in the future.

Chapter 6: Sleep Training Techniques

If you feel like you have tried everything but you are still not getting enough sleep, another option is to consider sleep training. There are many types, including gentle sleep methods to more formal sleep training. Some types of sleep training are controversial. This is because of what we know about infant sleep and the mismatch between what we do and what babies have evolved to expect. Sleep training can be considered trying to alter a baby's natural behaviour and by doing this it can have some consequences. You should therefore be fully informed about the advantages and disadvantages before deciding to implement sleep training with your own baby.

What is sleep training?

Sleep training is the process of teaching your child to fall asleep on his own and to go back to sleep (self soothe), if he wakes up in the middle of the night. It fosters a kind of independence that allows you to get more, much-needed rest so you can take better care of your baby and function normally in your day to day life.

Is sleep training a cure for my baby's sleep problems?

Sleep problems are often the difference between how a baby sleeps and how a parent wants a baby to sleep. Sleep is a developmental process. All babies will eventually learn to fall asleep and settle themselves when they wake, once they are biologically ready to do so. This is little consolation though, when you are dead on your feet with tiredness.

For exhausted parents with demanding lives and many pressures, sometimes extra help is needed to get their little one into an established sleep routine sooner than when nature intended. The good news is that with consistency and perseverance, sleep training can work.

Reminder! Sometimes parents think that their baby has a sleep problem when he wakes up several times during the night. This isn't the case, particularly for babies under six months old. Night waking is normal. Sleep training will not stop night waking but will help your child to learn to go back to sleep on his own when he does wake up.

When should you begin sleep training?

Some types of sleep training, such as the gentle sleep methods described below can begin once your baby has passed the fourth trimester. When your baby turns four months old, you may notice a more regular sleep-wake cycle, a drop in night feeds, and longer stretches of night sleep. These are signals that your baby may be ready for some of the gentle sleep training methods. Every baby is different so you can start the training earlier or later depending on when these signs become evident.

Like everything, when it comes to human behaviour, there is no 'one size fits all'. The same is true when it comes to sleep training. Every baby has his own temperament and what works for one family won't work for another. Remember that you know your baby better than anyone else. Trust your judgement and be confident in your ability to settle your baby.

When not to try sleep training?

Formal sleep training is not for every baby or family. If you are considering sleep training for your child, here are some reasons why you should avoid it this time:

- **Underlying medical conditions**: If you think your child has a medical problem, such as disruptive sleep or sleep apnea, consult your paediatrician first before starting a sleep training program.
- **Avoid major events**: A big work project, a house move, or a visit from family could make it difficult to stick to the training consistently. Rather than forcing it, wait until conditions at home become "normal" for at least two weeks for the sleep training to be effective.
- **Bed sharing or co-sleeping**: Sleep training is more difficult to do if you are co-sleeping or sharing a room with your child. If you are bed sharing, it becomes even more challenging. Before sleep training your child, you should first consider when and how to end co-sleeping.

Gentle sleep methods

Gentle sleep methods are recommended for babies from four months old.

1.The Bedtime Routine

As described in the chapter, "Preparing Your Baby For Sleep", introducing a calm bedtime routine is a common starting point for most parents with respect to sleep training. This method works well as it creates a relaxing routine for both parents and baby at the end of each day. It can be very flexible and combines well with other siblings.

If however, despite establishing a good bed time routine with calmness and consistency, your baby is still not settling down to sleep, waking frequently at night and not self-settling, you may wish to try another form of sleep training.

2.The Fading Method

Ideal for parents who want the training to be as gentle as possible, the goal of the fading method is to coach your baby to sleep on his own with very little crying involved. This approach involves gradually removing the sleep 'crutch' that keeps your baby from getting complete sleep, such as a bottle, the breast, or a pacifier or dummy.

How does it work?

On the first night, you offer the breast or bottle, but withdraw it when your baby falls asleep. If he cries, offer the breast or bottle again and repeat the process until your baby falls asleep without waking up when the breast or bottle is removed. During the following nights, withdraw the bottle or breast a little sooner, after feeding is complete but when he is still awake but drowsy.

The fading method is considered a kinder process since its goal is to help your baby become less and less dependent on the sleep crutch by withdrawing it sooner in each sleep period. Eventually, he learns to fall asleep on his own. Your child's temperament is a major factor in determining how long it takes for you to start seeing results with the fading method so you need to be pretty patient. Another factor you need to consider is your baby's age. The fading approach works faster with younger babies whose sleep associations aren't as persistent as in older ones.

Apart from a calm bedtime routine, the fading technique is considered the most gentle of the sleep training approaches as it involves the least amount of tears. It is the ideal solution if you want to be with your child every step of the way. It is also great if you practice attachment parenting, but want your baby to be independent when it comes to bedtime and sleeping. The fading method can be hard to maintain. It is a gradual approach and you need to be consistent each and every night, otherwise, your efforts will be wasted or it will take a long time to see results. As a consequence, many parents can become frustrated and give up before their baby learns to sleep on his own.

Attachment parenting: This is an approach to caring for babies and very young children that uses emotionally and physically responsive parenting. Key aspects include, breastfeeding, physical closeness, such as bed sharing and baby wearing and giving a lot of attention when babies cry or indicate they have other needs.

3.The "Pick-up-put-down" Method

Pick-up-put-down is a method popularized by Tracy Hogg in her book "The Baby Whisperer." Like the fading technique, it is a gentle sleep training solution that involves very little tears. While Tracy doesn't advocate letting babies cry it out, she believes that babies should learn to sleep without depending on sleep props or crutches like nursing, bottle-feeding, rocking, and similar activities.

How does it work?

As the name implies, pick-up-put-down involves picking up and comforting your baby when he fusses or cries in his crib at bedtime. When he's calm or drowsy, put him down. Keep repeating the process until your baby falls asleep on his own. You may use the "Four S" ritual of helping your child calm down: **S**etting the stage (bedtime routine), **S**waddling, **S**itting quietly with your baby, and **S**hush-pat. You can modify the steps involved in this ritual according to the age of your baby. For example, skip the swaddling part for older babies or babies who don't want to be swaddled. Tracy suggests that the pick-up-put-down method should be used for babies between four and eight months. For older babies, picking up would no longer be necessary. Instead, gently lay your baby down every time he sits up.

While this approach is a gentle method that minimises crying, it doesn't work for all babies. Some find the actions of being picked up and put down or being laid down whenever they sit up more stimulating than relaxing. Pick-up-put-down also requires patience on your part because you need to see the process to the end, which could take a while with some babies. To see results, you need to implement the method for two to three weeks, although some parents have had success more quickly. Again, it comes down to several factors which include your child's temperament, your own temperament and patience level as well as your own consistency.

The pick-up-put-down technique is a great solution if you don't want to leave your child alone and crying at any point during the training. But, it can be very demanding physically since night waking's can sometimes last more than two hours at the start, with many pick-ups. In fact, this method is better implemented with the assistance of another person so make sure you and your partner are on the same page before starting this sleep training option.

4.The "Camping Out" Method (also known as the "Chair Method")

Another form of gentle sleep training is the 'camping out' method. This method involves gradually withdrawing your presence from your baby's room at bedtime. The process consists of five steps: gently patting or rubbing your baby (physical contact), sitting by the crib, moving away from the crib but staying inside the room, staying by the door, and moving out of the room and into the hall. To make the 'camping out' strategy effective, keep interactions brief and minimal. It also helps if you use a script as a signal to your child that it's time for bed. For example, "It's time for bed. I love you. Good night," is something you could say to your baby every time you put him to bed. You can do this even if he is still too young to understand.

A variation of this sleep training technique is to have no interaction with your child as you are only in the room to reassure him with your presence. This method can be difficult and confusing, but according to parents who have found this technique to be effective, consistency and time helped them achieve the desired result.

Formal sleep training

Note: Formal sleep training methods are not recommended for babies under six months old.

The "Cry-it-out" Method

As the name implies, the cry-it-out sleep training technique involves crying (from the child and, sometimes, the parents). We know that babies are not able to settle themselves in to a state of calm without the help of a loving adult. They can become very distressed when left to cry alone. Over time, if no one comes to help them, they eventually go to sleep exhausted and stressed. It is not recommended that a baby is left for long periods in a state of distress. This can also be very upsetting for parents. However, this method can work for babies who only cry briefly before falling asleep. It is important to bear all this in mind if intending to use the 'cry it out' method.

The cry-it-out approach is divided into two categories which are graduated extinction and unmodified extinction. The name alone may strike fear in to the hearts of some parents but many have found success in this method of getting their baby to sleep better.

1.The Graduated Extinction Method, Ferber Method or 'Ferberizing'.

Graduated extinction, more popularly known as the Ferber method or Ferberizing, involves letting your child cry, then checking on him at specific intervals. For instance, if your child cries after putting him to bed, wait one minute before checking on him. If he cries again after you leave the room, wait two minutes before going back. Keep checking on him until he falls asleep but make sure to increase the intervals in between checks. Checking your child should also be timed, which should last around two to three minutes every time. As with the camping out method, if possible, interactions should be brief and without physical contact.

While graduated extinction can be quite an effective form of sleep training, it remains controversial since it still involves leaving a baby to cry. Researchers also agree that it is not appropriate for young babies under six months old. The sleeping patterns of young babies are still immature and are mostly influenced by their need to feed. Even expert proponents of gradual extinction or the Ferber method consider it inappropriate to sleep train babies who are younger than six months old.

2.The Unmodified Extinction Method

Unmodified extinction is a sleep training method that involves putting your child to bed at a specific time and leaving the room without checking on him. The idea behind this method is that the child will eventually stop crying and go to sleep on his own once he realizes that no one is going to come and comfort him. Understandably, many people struggle with this approach. However, there are still parents who report that unmodified extinction is a quick and effective method for sleep training if done the right way.

Dr Weissbluth, author of "Healthy Sleep Habits, Happy Child," is the most well-known advocate of unmodified extinction, although he also proposed a gradual extinction method similar to Ferberizing. For the purpose of clarity, unmodified extinction referred to in this guide is the Weissbluth method. While you will find many arguments against the cry-it-out approach in general, it's useful to understand the basics of Weissbluth's method of unmodified extinction to help you decide whether this strategy could work for your family or not.

Key aspects of the Weissbluth unmodified extinction method:

- The Weissbluth method is not intended for children below six months old. Feeding and nappy changes are the major reasons why younger children require more attention than older ones so you cannot just let your newborn cry it out.
- Applying the Weissbluth method does not mean your child will starve. In fact, it provides for one to two night feeds until your baby is nine months old. (In any case, night feeds would no longer be necessary for older babies as long as they are gaining weight and are otherwise healthy). If your baby is premature, make sure you discuss sleep training options with your doctor first.
- The Weissbluth method seems to require what is tantamount to ignoring your child. But, it actually involves taking note of your child's sleep cues and acting on that knowledge on time. If you act on the sleep cues in time, your baby should be able to fall asleep without too many tears.
- Contrary to Ferberizing, Weissbluth's unmodified extinction takes your child's temperament into account while sleep training. You can modify the approach as you see fit based on your baby's personality.
- The cry-it-out strategy does require parents to put their baby to bed at bedtime and leave them. However, this

doesn't mean you can't perform soothing techniques before then. Rocking your baby until he is drowsy is one of the suggestions provided in the Weissbluth Paediatrics website. Just make sure your child doesn't become dependent on these and remember to be firm about bedtime.

- Some argue that the Ferber method of constantly checking on your child can make him more upset. It could also reinforce the crying and make it last longer than in the Weissbluth method of not checking on your child at all.
- Developing healthy sleep habits in young babies and children is paramount, according to Weissbluth. The ultimate goals of his approach are to remove any sleep associations and to teach your little one to self-soothe. As such, the method makes considerations for special situations, such as when your child is sick, has had a nightmare, or has wet his bed.

The downside of leaving your baby to cry

Many parents are uncomfortable with the cry-it-out method and science provides reasons why it's not for everyone. Keep in mind, though, that these reasons are based on the application of the cry-it-out approach in general and not just when sleep training.

- Babies cannot soothe themselves under intense distress because their brains are not yet developed enough to do this. Moreover, extreme agitation without comfort produces cortisol, which in high enough quantities damages neurons or nerve connections in the brain. This is crucial in the first year of the child's life since the brain grows three times in size during this period.
- Infants communicate their needs through crying and a parent's instinct is to respond to those cries. If the baby is left to cry, his stress levels mirror that of his mother's. But when the crying stops because the baby is not

getting any response, the mother's stress levels go back to normal but the baby's remains high.

- Babies don't learn to self-regulate on their own, they take cues from their parents who hold and comfort them when they are distressed. They use this information when they need to self-soothe. Leaving babies to cry alone repeatedly and for extended periods will only teach them that the world is a lonely, loveless place.
- A mother and her baby are connected in an intuitive way, such that the mother eventually understands what her child needs just by hearing a whimper or a cry. If she trains herself to ignore her baby's cries, she could lose this connection and might find it hard to identify and respond to the child's needs in the long run.

The list of arguments for and against the unmodified and gradual extinction provided in this guide is not exhaustive. It is recommended that your read more about the Ferber and Weissbluth approaches to sleep training before making a decision about using this technique.

Which sleep training method is best?

Researchers and sleep experts are still divided on the subject of which sleep training approach is best, but what most of them agree on is the importance of consistency. Based on a review of fifty two sleep studies published in the Sleep journal, almost all the various approaches were effective when consistently applied.

Hence, choose a training method that you can follow through and would work well with your baby's personality and your own. Timing is crucial as well because once you start the training, you should keep at it every night for at least a week (depending on the method, your baby, and other conditions). Moreover, when you review the various sleep training techniques, you will see that many of them highlight the importance of watching out for your baby's sleep cues, acting on them in a timely manner, and performing bedtime rituals.

No sleep training approach is perfect since each child is unique. Use your gut feel as well as your knowledge of your baby when choosing the best method for your family. You could also combine several methods to see what works. As long as the approach is effective for your baby and your family, keep doing it. If the technique you chose doesn't seem to be working or it seems to have had a negative effect overall, stop it. After a few weeks, try the method again or use a different approach. Finally, expect relapses (despite previous success) with a sleep training technique when your child gets sick, reaches a new milestone, or when major changes (such as a vacation, moving to a new house, and so on) take place. When this happens, gradually reinstate the training once everything is back to normal.

While sleep training is a foreign concept in other parts of the world, it is quite common in the US. In fact, it is necessary if parents hope to sleep more than four hours every night, or if the mother expects to go back to work after giving birth. On the subject of maternity leave, the US has one of the shortest in the world - twelve weeks. The leave is also unpaid, causing mothers to return to the workplace as soon as possible.

According to an article in Psychology Today (www.psychologytoday.com), formal sleep training methods are not natural and are detrimental to a baby's health. However, the author also points out in the same post, parents in the US are usually away from their extended families who would otherwise help with the childrearing. Because lack of sleep has serious consequences on physical and mental health as well as relationships, sleep training is seen as a way for parents (and their children) to get more sleep. The US health department and academies even advise parents to sleep train their children. Note that this advice prioritises the needs of parents over the needs of babies.

In addition, to help resolve these sleep issues, parents are looking more and more to 'sleep specialists' or 'sleep consultants'. The sleep consulting industry is unregulated, which raises concerns about the credentials of the consultants as well as the effects of their methods. These services can also be expensive for a family on an average income. Is it sensible therefore to check references thoroughly or get word of mouth recommendations before committing to these services.

Whether in the US, or in other parts of the world, sleep training remains a controversial topic that has parents, caregivers, health care providers, psychologists, and sleep experts divided.

At the end of the day, you should decide whether sleep training is for you, your baby and your family. If you do decide to use sleep training make sure you are comfortable with the method you choose and monitor closely how your baby is reacting to it. If in any doubt seek advice from a health professional.

Key summary points – sleep training techniques

First three months or fourth trimester

Due to your baby's stage of development he needs to sleep, wake and feed regularly during a twenty four hour period. Any sleep training attempted at this point is likely to be unsuccessful. If you can, make life easy on yourself by keeping life simple and going with the flow for a while.

From **three to six months** the following gentle sleep methods are suitable:

1. Bedtime routine
2. Fading method
3. Pick up put down method
4. Camping out or chair method

From **six months onwards** the following sleep methods can be tried:

1. Bedtime routine
2. Fading method
3. Pick up put down method
4. Camping out or chair method
5. Cry it out – Graduated extinction or Ferber Method
6. Cry it out – Unmodified extinction or Weissbluth Method

My experience

In the early weeks after my son's birth, I began a simple bed time routine. This consisted mainly of a warm bath or a 'top and tail' wash for him, then a change in to a clean sleepsuit for bed time. Because I was so exhausted by that time of day, I often sat on the sofa with the TV on giving him a last feed. As I was breastfeeding, this often went on for ages as each time I tried to move him to his cot, he wakened up again and wanted to reattach to me! By the time he was three months old I was really needing more sleep and decided to try the fading method. My own tiredness and resulting frustration meant that I had mixed success with this method. I was also unaware that my mood would affect how settled my baby would be. This resulted in me often taking him in to my bed with me. Things did get easier as he got older and by six months I had moved him in to his own room next door to me. By this age, he was much more active during the day and beginning to eat solids with the result that naturally, he was ready for bed and slept longer.

Chapter 7: Take Control by Creating a Sleep Plan

The previous chapters have hopefully helped you to better understand your baby's stages of sleep development and how he views the world. Understanding the positive impact you have on your baby when you are calm and relaxed is very important. You now know the best ways to soothe, settle and prepare your baby for sleep and how to create a safe sleep environment. You have also now considered parenting styles, schedule types and sleep training options.

This combined knowledge should greatly increase your confidence around making informed decisions about how best to care for your baby. This is much better than making choices based on the 'route of least resistance' when you are exhausted. The next step in the journey is to build a new strategy, take control and finally achieve the goal – to get more sleep. A great way to do this is to create a sleep plan.

What is a sleep plan?

A sleep plan is essentially a list of preferences, wishes, roles and responsibilities relating to the sleeping arrangements and behaviours around your baby's sleep. Once you decide on your plan, you should write it down and pin it up somewhere easy to see. You can refer to it whenever you are extremely tired or having a really tough night and don't know what to do. It can be especially useful when you are wakened from a deep sleep at three am and feel very disorientated and groggy. It also prevents disagreement about whose turn it is to settle the baby or get up first in the morning. When you are very tired everything seems more difficult therefore the plan should

71

be clear but flexible. The plan is designed to help you feel more in control and be a guide when you are too tired to make decisions. It is not designed to make you feel guilty if you aren't able to follow it all of the time. It is important that if you have a partner, the plan should be created and agreed between you. Your plan can be shared with all those involved in your baby's care including grandparents, nursery staff or nannies. This way, a consistent approach is taken, with respect to your baby's sleep that is fully approved by you.

Sleep plan timing

There is no best time to develop a sleep plan however, it is likely to be much more successful once your baby has passed the fourth trimester. It is easier if you can stay relaxed and 'go with the flow', for first few months. Your situation may dictate that you need a plan earlier than this. If so, don't set your expectations too high and be realistic about what you can achieve. At this early stage, you are unlikely to be able to change your baby's behaviour. You can choose to change your own behaviour though, and making this the focus of a sleep plan with a newborn baby, will be more successful.

How to create a sleep plan

It is simple to create a sleep plan. A good place to start is by talking with your partner or a family member about your individual parenting style. Lots of things influence your parenting style and it helps to discuss your views on sleep routines early on or even better, before your baby is born. One of the biggest influences on how we parent our children is how we were parented ourselves. If your partner had very relaxed parents without strict bedtimes and you grew up with lots of rules, it is important that you acknowledge your different experiences and agree a new way forward together. Life can get very stressful if you both have very different ideas about how to parent – particularly when it comes to sleep routines. If you are a single parent, you will only have your own views to consider but it can still be helpful to talk through your ideas with someone who is also a parent. Try not to be influenced by fashion or what your peers are doing. Listen to your gut about what is right for you and your baby. You know your own baby best.

Here are some other questions to guide your thinking. Noting down your answers will help shape your sleep plan.

1. What is your parenting style and how does this influence your views on sleep?
2. What type of daily schedule would work for you and your family?
3. What are your views on the best sleep habits?
4. What are you views on having your baby in bed with you?
5. Pacifiers/dummies – yes/no/maybe?
6. Leave baby to cry or pick up right away?
7. What things can you do to catch up on sleep when necessary?
8. How will you support each other when things get tough?

Once you have discussed the questions and your answers with your partner, agree the principles of the plan. (It will differ depending on the age and stage of your baby). Write down what is most important to you both first. As an example, - bedtime is at 7pm every night. Add in other things that you agree on. You may want to assign certain tasks to each other such as partner gives baby his bath when possible.

Having a Plan A (your ideal) for when things are going well is great but you should also have a Plan B to fall back on when things are going a bit pear shaped such as asking your mother in law to come over! You can make it as detailed or as simple as a few bullet points. It's your plan for you to use and feel good about. The overall outcome needed is to have a plan that you both agree on, then try out, modify and repeat as needed.

Implementing your master plan

The person implementing the plan should be as calm and relaxed as possible. It will always be harder to settle your baby if you are tense and upset. Keep in mind, your baby has no knowledge of how tired or busy you are. Make things easy on yourself by having your baby sleep set up ready for both daytime naps and bedtime with bedding changes available if required. Expect some change as your baby grows. The first year of your baby's life brings about many milestones. Growth spurts can easily throw him off his routine as these can be accompanied by an increased need to feed and sleep, amongst other things. Adjust your plan to accommodate these changes. For example, if your baby keeps falling asleep during feeding and is unable to fuel up enough for the night, switch feeding to an earlier time in your routine. Be consistent where possible as this helps your baby to learn what to expect next. Finally, give your plan time to work. It may take a week or two for your baby to adjust to the new routine so don't give up if you don't see immediate changes in behaviour.

Celebrate success

Rather than feel down about your situation, choose to celebrate any and all success. Perhaps your baby took a longer nap or was quicker to settle than normal. Maybe you recognised his sleep cue and acted in time. See each small success as a step in the right direction. Even if you are only chinking your mug of tea (or strong black coffee!) with your partner or friend or drawing a smiley face or star on your sleep plan, give yourself a pat on the back for this achievement. As each day passes, you are creating memories that will last forever. Make these great memories by focusing on the positive. Give each other support and encouragement whenever possible and remember you are doing your very best.

Top tips for sleep plan success

1. If you have a partner, create the plan together.
2. Keep it simple. You are more likely to follow it.
3. Know your plan. Pin up copies in easy to read places.
4. Believe in your plan - it will work!
5. Establish new routines slowly.
6. Give it time to work.
7. Don't expect too much if starting your plan during the fourth trimester.
8. Try to be consistent but equally, don't be hard on yourself (or your partner) if you don't keep to the plan all the time.
9. Review your plan regularly and adjust as your baby grows.
10. Share your plan with all those involved with your baby's sleep routine.
11. Celebrate any and all successes – even small ones!

Share your plan to share the load

If life is feeling out of control and everyone is exhausted and grumpy, making a sleep plan will really help. Creating a sleep plan is an easy way to make your life easier with a young baby. It will help you to feel you have some control back over your situation and will allow you to ask for help when necessary. It serves as a guide to fall back on when you're too tired or sleepy to make decisions and also clarifies who is responsible for different tasks. Making your plan available to others who are involved in the care of your baby such as grandparents or aunts and uncles will ensure everyone is clear about your baby's sleep routine and arrangements. If you have other children, they can also be included in the plan so that everyone takes a share in helping the new little person settle in to your unique family routine.

Ready to create your own sleep plan?

Make it easy on yourself and download a copy of our step by step Sleep Plan Template.

Go to http://bestwellbeingbooks.com/sleeping-baby-happy-parents/

Chapter 8: Quick Fix Sleep Solutions

It's good to remember, it is completely normal for babies to wake regularly during the first few months. This will not change until they grow, mature and develop.

However sometimes you just need sleep and fast. It's easy to get very caught up in your baby's sleep needs, but your wellbeing is every bit as important and making good choices on how to get sleep does help a lot. Suggestions to look at are below, some of the ideas need a little planning but many can be implemented immediately.

Once you get yourself sorted and feeling in control, check out some of the quick fix ideas to settle your little one too.

A word of caution, don't try them all at once. Although you will want an instant result, your baby will take time to adjust to a new situation or stimulus so don't rush this. Try one thing at a time and see if it works for your baby. Score each quick fix out of ten, depending on how successful they are. This will give you your top five 'go to' sleep techniques. Remember, as your baby grows, different techniques may work so it's worth retrying some at a later date.

Check through the parent quick fixes first.

Parent quick fixes

Give yourself permission to take a break.
Sometimes when things get tough, you and your baby need a break from each other. Another pair of hands to bear the load can make all the difference, so don't be afraid to ask for help when you need it. If you are on your own and feeling at the end of your tether, lay your baby down safely in his bed, and go to another room. Use the techniques at the end of Chapter one to help you calm yourself before you return to your baby

Hire a baby sitter.
If you really need some sleep, and fast, and you don't have friends and family available to help, why not pay a sitter for a few hours? It could make all the difference for a small investment.

Sleep when your baby sleeps.
However short each nap may be, it helps you reduce the sleep debt that has been piling up since birth. If you're worried that you won't hear your baby when he cries, don't worry. You're programmed to hear him if you're in the same room. Otherwise, you can get a baby monitor.

Bed-share.
When planned and done safely, following the bed sharing advice, having your baby in bed with you can give you much needed sleep. There is no doubt it's where you baby wants to be, snuggled by your side. It' s not for everyone but it certainly does work.

Enlist the help of others.
Most partners expect that they need to help with the baby, but sometimes they don't know exactly what needs to be done. Be specific about the tasks and be appreciative so they will be motivated to help out more. Accept offers of help from other friends and family, even if it's just to receive a home cooked meal or get help with the laundry.

Limit visitors.
In the early weeks, limit home visitors. These visits may be welcome at first but a continuous parade of callers is exhausting and could put additional pressure on you to clean the house and entertain even if you don't feel like doing so. This can also be too much for your baby.

Get short-term help.
Having someone you can rely on to cook, clean, do the laundry, and run errands is something you will greatly appreciate. In some cultures, parents and relatives come and live-in, providing practical help and support for many months after the arrival of a new baby. If you are not so lucky, make life as easy as possible by using online grocery shopping, eating simple, quickly prepared or ready meals and relaxing your household standards for a little while. Consider hiring a cleaner for a few months to take the pressure off. You are definitely worth it!

Take a break from household chores.
At this time, the well-being of your infant and yourself is the highest priority, so don't worry too much about a sink full of dirty dishes or the overflowing laundry hamper. Deal with them when you have the energy or have someone do the chores for you.

Try to relax.
Although you are exhausted and desperate for sleep, you may find falling asleep difficult. This can be caused by a number of different things. You may be physically exhausted but your mind won't switch off. This can be linked to worry and anxiety about your baby, particularly if there are health issues or he was born prematurely. Following the safe sleeping guidelines and having your baby in the same room as you can help. Lack of sleep over a period of time is unhealthy so it's important to address this. Chapter one suggests ways to help yourself relax, but get additional support if you need it, keep in mind this phase will not last long and will pass.

Baby quick fixes

Just like adults, babies receive stimulation and messages from all of their senses. As adults, if any of our senses become overwhelmed, we are able to move away or stop the stimulation. For example, you can walk away from loud noises or take a layer of clothing off when you are too hot. Your baby relies entirely on you to do this for him. He tells you he is uncomfortable through his body movements and other 'cues'. If you don't pick these up, he starts to cry.

While trying to settle him, thinking about each of your baby's senses and what is happening in that moment is useful. You can do this quickly and without much effort. Even making small changes and adjustments could make all the difference.

Below are some questions and ideas to help you think this through.

Sight - *Stop and think about what your baby can see.*

> **Can he see you?** Some strollers, buggy's and pushchairs have the baby facing away from his parent. Does your baby prefer to see you in his vision? It may make him feel safer to see that you are near.

> **Are you smiling and happy? Or cross and grumpy?** Your baby focuses on your facial expressions and can pick up your mood very easily. Check your facial expression in the mirror. How do you feel looking at your own expression?

> **Is it too bright?** Although you may enjoy a lovely, sunny day, it may be too bright for your baby. Always protect his eyes from bright sunlight. If you are putting down to sleep, he may prefer a darker

room. Consider black out blinds to keep natural light out if necessary. For a quick fix, try pining a thick towel over the window and see if this makes any difference.

Bored of the view? A change of scenery is often enough to calm a crying infant. If it's too cold, try going to a different room in the house instead and look out the window together. The point is to distract your baby by changing the environment and stop the crying.

Sound - *Stop and listen to the sounds around you.*

What tone of voice are you using? It is awfully difficult to consistently use a loving, calm tone of voice when you are exhausted and very fed up. However, speaking softly and gently to your baby will always be more effective in calming him rather than using an angry tone.

Is it too quiet or too noisy? Background noise seems to settle some babies. Try playing the radio quietly. If it's too quiet, they might think they are alone. Loud bangs or unexpected noises will startle your baby (just like adults). Try to minimise these. Playgrounds, soft play areas and nurseries can also be very noisy for a young baby.

Shushing sounds can work: If you are in bed, you don't always have to get up to feed, or rock your baby to sleep every time he cries or stirs in the middle of the night. Sometimes shushing is enough to calm and soothe him since it mimics the sounds your baby heard inside the womb. You can also pat his little bottom gently while making shushing sounds.

Play music or sing: Babies love to hear their parent's calm voices and are often soothed by them singing. Did you sing to your baby during pregnancy? If so, try those same songs. Perhaps there was a music playlist you enjoyed during pregnancy or a relaxation audio. Try playing this to your baby. You may be surprised how effective it is at calming your baby, and you.

Try white noise: Many parents swear by white noise to soothe their baby. Examples such as hair dryers, washing machines and vacuum cleaners are popular choices. It's worth a try!

Touch – *Take a moment to think about how much recent holding and handling your baby has had.*

Babies feel safest when they are in contact or very close to you. Being close to your calm body helps them feel calm. Equally, too much handling or being passed around from one person to the next can have the opposite effect and make your baby unsettled.

A lovely cuddle: Maybe your baby just needs you to help calm him down. Hold him close to your chest and gently rock, pat or stroke him.

Give some space: If the world around your baby has been very busy, he may just need some peace and quiet. Lay him down gently in his familiar sleep place and give him some space to recover.

Kangaroo care or 'skin to skin': While recommended for premature babies, kangaroo care benefits even full-term babies. To do this, undress you baby and place him against your naked skin. Then, use a soft, warm blanket to cover you both. Aside from encouraging longer and deeper sleep, kangaroo care can help regulate the baby's heart rate and breathing as well as improve the mother's milk production. Skin to skin can also be down by partners and works very well too.

Swaddling: The womb is a snug and cozy environment that you can replicate by swaddling your infant. Swaddling keeps babies from jerking or getting startled violently while asleep so it can make your baby's slumber deeper and longer. However, you should be aware of the guidance for safe swaddling:

1. Don't wrap your baby too tightly.
2. Don't constrict your baby's hips and allow enough space for him to bend his knees.
3. Keep your baby on his back while swaddled.
4. Prevent him from overheating by; not covering his head, using clothes and a swaddling blanket of the appropriate material and thickness.

Baby-wearing: Because babies love close contact, (especially with their mothers), many swear by baby wearing. Ideal for the first few months to help babies sleep soundly, baby wearing also helps soothe a colicky or fussy baby. This is great for dads and other family members too, making them feel included.

Massaging: Massages are not only good for the baby's digestion and growth, as well as overall development, it also allows them to sleep more easily and soundly. Additionally, it provides a great bonding opportunity for you and your baby.

A warm bath: As adults we often find a warm bath relaxing and the same can work for your baby. Even better is to get in the bath together and enjoy skin to skin contact. This can be very relaxing for you both. Make sure the water is not too hot (just above body temperature is correct). Only try this if there is another adult present who can take your baby from you when you are ready to get out of the bath.

Movement - *Has your baby been lying still for a while or maybe he needs to be still?*

> **Rocking**: Parents instinctively rock their babies. It is naturally very soothing as the motion mimics the movements in the womb. Although rocking can be very effective, it quickly becomes tiring for a sleepy parent. Rocking chairs can work as long as you don't fall asleep too. Alternatively try laying your baby in his pram or stroller and pushing it back and forth on the spot.

> **Go for a walk:** Fresh air is great for your baby, so go out and take a walk even for just a few minutes during the day. Studies show that young infants who are taken outside during the afternoons sleep better and longer than those who aren't.

Swinging: The rhythmic motion of a swing can help calm and soothe some babies. Make sure to use the appropriate size and type of swing seat for your baby's age. Note: check whether your baby likes the sensation of swinging before buying a swing seat. (My son hated the sensation and cried even more!)

Smell - *Babies have sensitive noses and don't like strong, overpowering smells.*

> **Do you notice any strong smells?** As adults, we can become immune or 'used to' some powerful smells such as some home air freshener, household and other highly fragranced products. Ask someone else to check if you don't have a sensitive nose.

Babies prefer familiar smells: The smell of you and your home are all soothing smells for your baby. The smell of his own bed is comforting so if you are planning a trip away, it can help to take his bedding or sleeper sack with you. Some babies find the scent of essential oils calming. Use these sparingly in a diffuser.

Taste and sucking – *Babies have a strong sucking reflex from birth and find sucking very soothing.*

Try a pacifier or dummy: While many people are still on the fence about using a pacifier, the American Academy of Pediatrics (AAP) suggests that giving a newborn a pacifier is perfectly fine. Your baby may be one of many who have strong sucking needs that can be quickly soothed by a pacifier.

Hungry: Babies need to feed regularly so, unless he has had a feed very recently, offer the bottle or breast to check he is not hungry. If you are concerned about any aspect of feeding, check with your health professional or breastfeeding counsellor for advice.

Physical

Check his temperature: Young babies can't regulate their body temperature, so make sure your baby isn't too hot or too cold by checking his clothing as well as the temperature inside the room/house. Note: Check the temperature of his back or tummy rather than his hands and feet as they tend to be cooler.

Check for illness: If, despite your best efforts, your baby is fretful, unhappy and hard to settle, it's important to ensure that he is not unwell. Not all symptoms of illness are obvious so get him checked out by your Doctor if you are not sure. Seek a second opinion if necessary. The purple crying website can also provide additional information - www.purplecrying.info.

The top 5 that worked well for me were:

1. Movement and rocking – putting my baby in the pram and going for a walk outside or pushing it back and forth, gently in the hallway.
2. Swaddling and laying him down in a quiet spot with minimum stimulation.
3. Cuddling up (safely) on the bed together for a nap.
4. Giving a warm bath (once past the newborn stage).
5. Singing many made up versions of the 'Wheels on the bus', over and over in a quiet, calm voice.

Chapter 9: Conclusion

Reading this book and following some of the tips and guidance should have helped you and your baby to get a good night's sleep. Good sleep is fundamental to your physical and mental wellbeing. Sleeping Baby, Happy Parents includes all the key information you need to make confident parenting choices.

The book began by focusing on you, and your wellbeing, which is so important when caring for a baby. Next we explored your baby's experience and perspective of life so far. We described how much your little human's environment has changed from womb to world, and it has changed a lot! We considered parenting styles and gave options of the kind of parent you might want to be. This was followed by looking at how to create a great sleep environment that is both safe and conducive to your baby's needs. This set the scene for good naps and great night time sleep.

Preparing your baby for sleep, understanding sleep cues, soothing your baby and creating routines were all explored allowing you to pick and try what would work best for you. Sleep training can be a controversial subject. We described the most widely accepted techniques in order to allow you to select the type to suit your parenting style best. The creation of a good sleep plan is key to you and your baby getting good quality sleep. The plan works best if it is created, agreed and implemented by you and your partner together as a team.

The parent and baby quick fix sleep solutions in the last chapter provided ideas and tips on what to do for you and your baby in order to quickly get some precious sleep if things get a little out of control.

I wrote this book to make other parent's life's easier and help them to spend more time enjoying having a young baby. I spent over ten years as an antenatal teacher supporting expectant and new parents while being mum to three children. During this time, I built up a lot of knowledge and experience and also found many sources of information that I wanted to share. I hope that I have brought all of this together in a concise, easy to read format to help you find the best way to get your baby to sleep (especially when you are tired!)

Being a parent should be the most wonderful time in your life. Having a young baby is a very short phase and should be enjoyed while it lasts. You will only enjoy it if you are getting enough sleep. Reading this book will have provided all you need to know to make the right choices for you to get more sleep. This will help create great memories of this precious time which are lovely to reflect on when the teenage years kick in!

Did you find this book helpful?

I would be very grateful if you could share your experience and help other parents by leaving a review at either:

Amazon US:

http://amzn.to/2ys3oul

Amazon UK:

http://amzn.to/2ztPFmN

Other related books by this author:

About the author

Emma Thomson

Emma is a mother and business professional, educated in human resources, childbirth and biochemistry. Emma is a keen author and has written a number of books on pregnancy, parenthood and people development subjects. She wants to share her knowledge to help new and existing parents relax and better enjoy the gift of parenthood.

Acknowledgements

Thank you to Sally-Anne Holman for her advice and guidance on the content of this book. Sally-Anne's qualifications include a Higher National Diploma in Antenatal education and a Postgraduate certificate in Adult Education and Training. She is also a Doula UK recognised birth and postnatal doula.

24430971R00057

Printed in Great Britain
by Amazon